Developing a Corporate Identity

Developing a Corporate Identity
How to Stand Out in the Crowd

Elinor Selame
Joe Selame

CHAIN STORE AGE BOOKS
An Affiliate of Lebhar-Friedman, Inc., New York

Developing a Corporate Identity: How to Stand Out in the Crowd

Printed in the United States of America
Library of Congress Catalog Card Number: 74-23015
International Standard Book Number: 0-912016-34-5

Acknowledgments

The information, case studies, and illustrations in this book were made available for inclusion only because so many individuals, companies, and organizations answered our letters of inquiry, consented to interviews, and sent us the material that we requested. Although they are too numerous to mention here, much of the material received from them is incorporated into the text. We thank them for it collectively.

A special thanks to our assistant, Hollis Bruckner, who, in addition to her other work, served as typist and sounding board for the book, and to Patrice Sobin, our editor, who methodically, concisely, and creatively pulled the manuscript together.

Contents

Introduction

A 1972 Harris poll showed that 60 percent of the United States buying public does not trust American business. These consumers felt that they were not receiving value for their money.

According to a White House conference on the U.S. economy, "one out of five consumers feels cheated or deceived in the following: misleading advertising, faulty product, poor service, deceptive packaging, overcharging."

Surprisingly, a company might not be guilty of any of these offenses, but its image can project shoddy goods, unfair prices, sloppy service, lack of imagination, and dreariness. Store image is shaped by its merchandise, price range, name, trademark, house colors, interior and exterior architecture, advertising, packaging, and the way these are visually expressed. These elements can be controlled through a planned corporate identity program to project a favorable image in the minds of the buying public. Corporate identity does not change the facts, but it should reflect them accurately and precisely.

Decisions on the retail position in the marketplace are executive decisions. Because corporate identification is a visual reflection of a company's policies and objectives, an identity program should be planned and controlled by top management. However, before the public can be expected to know a company, the company must first know itself. Many times, the need to explain the company to a committee planning a new corporate identity properly brings into focus the desired image. Whatever the desired image is, it is essential that all elements are carefully controlled. The psychological satisfaction (or lack of it) a shopper receives during his visit to a store could be a major factor in his decision to buy or not and then in his decision to return.

This book attempts to provide specific information on the various elements of corporate identity, and is illustrated with case studies of projects as they answer specific identity problems. How identity problems can be alleviated or avoided altogether will be examined in depth.

The information presented should be read by anyone concerned with the identity of any business—top decision makers, planners, designers, advertising executives and outside advertising people, graphic designers, architects, and public relations people. They should know that they are involved in an identity program, what their responsibility is within that program, and what they are expected to do to maintain the image.

With thought and planning, any company can become truly distinctive and stand out from the crowd of its competitors.

chapter 1

A New Corporate Identity

WHAT IS CORPORATE IDENTITY?

If we speak to those in public relations, they might say that a corporate image is established through annual reports, employee newsletters, news releases for the public, feature articles, the smiles on employee's faces, and community relations. They are right. Advertising agencies will define the corporate image primarily as the company message that comes across through printed and broadcasted advertisements, brochures, and billboards. They are right. Architects will vouch for the importance of the structural appearance, and competent corporate designers and planners will understand this. They are right. For some firms, the corporate image might also be formed by packaging, traffic engineering, and landscaping. All these factors have positive or detrimental effects on how well a company is thought of. The *corporate image* is composed of all planned and unplanned verbal and visual elements that emanate from the corporate body and leave an impression on the observer.

The *corporate identity*, although it is one of the major influences on the corporate image, is all planned and all visual. A successful identity system visually separates and distinguishes a firm from its competitors. The corporate identity is the firm's visual statement to the world of who and what the company is—of how the company views itself—and therefore has a great deal to do with how the world views the company.

The major element of the corporate identity is the corporate symbol because it is the visible, easily recognizable face of a living, complex business machine. It allows the public to see who produces the goods or services they are buying and is therefore the foundation upon which corporate identity is built. The symbol becomes the focal rallying point of the corporation. It is the banner under which a president gathers his employees to meet the public.

It is most important to remember that *planned* corporate identity should reflect and communicate planned management policies. If an operation is not planning to provide service but plans to base its success on low price, then store identity should make this fact clear. To reflect this discount pricing policy, it is important not to have a luxurious decor. It is not necessary to look like a warehouse; in fact, many discounters feel that a "plain Jane" look is no longer necesssary to make their policies clear to the public. Clean, contemporary, simple design looks attractive yet gets the message across. Elaborate design does not reflect the same image. The store must reflect the difference between its prices and those of other retailers, if that is the selling point.

Management decides whether to build an image of high, low, medium, or mixed price and quality merchandise. The store's identity should reflect this. For example, it is one thing to carry expensive goods with service and beautiful decor, another to carry expensive goods at lower prices, minus the service and decor. It is one thing to price products below the usual market price, another to carry lower-quality goods at low price. There is room in the marketplace for all concepts, if positioned properly and creatively. However, the policies must be communicated honestly, or the company's image will quickly turn sour.

The presentation is the core, and the presentation becomes the image. A company is insulting the public unless it puts forth its best image. Business has an obligation to look well dressed—to its stockholders, to its employees, to its customers, and to the community.

WHY HAVE A CORPORATE IDENTITY PROGRAM?

One of the first identity goals of any commercial enterprise is to be seen and then remembered. In today's fast-paced, heavily populated society, to be seen and remembered is half the business battle. It is the faceless nature of many of our corporations that confuses and irritates the consumer. The public wants to know as much about you as you want to know about them. They want to know what it is that distinguishes your company from others. In what ways are you different?

A company's visual communication material is an expression of that corporation's philosophy, abilities, and culture. It can announce or mumble, inform or confuse, delight or depress, stimulate or irritate, and make a sale or break a sale. It is therefore very important for every company to plan these materials carefully. Planned corporate identity has the potential to make tomorrow's business something more than an accident.

Once the corporate identity is established through careful thought and with expertise and skill, it should be instituted as a long-range communication plan. As with any long-term business plan, it should allow for disciplined yet flexible changes and growth. When the overall corporate identity system is put into action, no more valuable time will be wasted on "crash" corporate-level communication decisions because guidelines for every detail will be available. The chief executive will be secure in knowing that the various representative materials carrying the company's banner are impressive, organized, proud looking, and truly representative of the firm's attitudes and objectives.

In the past, businesses have usually left the design of their products to engineers, the design of their factories and stores to several architects or contractors, their advertising to advertising firms, their letterhead and business cards to printers, their packaging and signs to suppliers, and so on. Each one, doing his best to get across the identity of the business as he saw it through the medium of his art, would develop a different corporate identification. When a top executive was not happy with one or all of these separate impressions, he would often waste valuable time with the printer or architect trying to get his ideas across. Because the supplier knew nothing about the company's corporate objectives, the solution they arrived at could be short-range at best. A well-planned, well-executed corporate identity program would obviate these problems.

It is important to the contemporary business community and to the individual business to have its contributions and attitudes accurately reflected. A sampling of Illinois adults showed that they thought: (1) business makes too much profit; (2) most advertising is dishonest; (3) products have deteriorated in quality over the past five or ten years; and (4) most large companies lack humanistic personal feelings toward their buying public.[1] Some of these feelings are not justified, as most business executives know. To counteract these feelings, the Illinois Chamber of Commerce launched a state-wide program entitled "Stand up for Business." Any company can launch its own program to counteract or prevent similar feelings: a corporate identity program that honestly communicates what and at what price and with what services it is offering for public consumption.

Research has shown that a company with a good corporate image has an ace in the hole with the consuming public. A study by Batten, Barton, Durstine & Osborn showed the following results:

1. When a company has a good image, the public is more likely to assume that it produces good products.

2. The public is more likely to pay more for a company's products and buy their new products if the company has a good image.

3. The public is more likely to take the company's side in disputes.

4. The public is more likely to consider the company's stock a good investment, and the stock is likely to suffer less in a general market decline than will the stock of a company that does not have as good an image.[2]

WHO SOULD BE IN CHARGE?

Implementing, administrating, and supervising a new identity program is not a job for the fainthearted. The person responsible for this job must be knowledgeable in the total scope of the company's communications and must be a good tactician. He must be capable of dealing with the human and complex needs of the various departments whose programs will be affected by the new visual identity. A new identity program will not only affect architecture, signage, interiors, packaging, advertising, internal and external graphic communications, and public

[1]   According to the "Illinois State Chamber of Commerce Public Opinion Survey of Attitudes Toward Business" (Chicago, Ill: Illinois State Chamber of Commerce, 1973). These facts are also published in a booklet entitled, "If Business is Your Bag . . . Say So—Out Loud."

[2]   From the 1969 *BBDO Research Report*, Research Department of Batten, Barton, Durstine & Osborn, Inc., New York, New York.

relations; it will also affect such other departments as accounting, which will have to deal with the implementation costs, the legal department, which will have to deal with trademark law, and so on.

A senior executive must be in command so that the program achieves the proper results in every department. This executive could be called the Keeper of the Mark, as he will have to see that the program is adhered to at every level. In a large firm, this is naturally a full-time job. In smaller companies, it can be an added function for the director of corporate communications, advertising director, public relations director, or marketing director. These executives, of course, should be aided by a design consultant (from the company if there is one, from outside the company if necessary) in the actual planning of any identity program. At the outset, they work together, and their plans are put into an identity manual, which then serves as their guide for the long-run program. Because the identity, once planned, will last, the manual must be as flexible as the program itself.

HOW TO SPOT IDENTITY PROBLEMS

If a company presents a dated or disorganized image, its best friends probably will not say so, and its competitors certainly will not. There are several danger signals that can be looked for, and if any of these signals apply, the company either has or will have an identity problem.

The first step in spotting a poorly defined identity is to appoint someone in the firm to collect all visual media being used by the corporation and its divisions: stationery, direct mailing pieces, billing forms, checks, statements, photos of on-site and remote signage, photos of vehicle identity, advertisements, and packages. Mount all these materials on large, 20-inch by 30-inch boards and check the following danger signals against this composite of the company.

1. The company is growing fast and furiously internally and through mergers and acquisitions. Each change is represented by a different look, so the composite shows a group of unrelated materials. Each time a change takes place, the top executives are presented with design decisions concerning names, trademarks, letterheads, and so on; and the decisions have been made independently of previous decisions. Most outsiders and some insiders are therefore surprised when they are told about all the divisions of the

company. They do not realize that it is so large and diversified; they cannot tell from the communication materials.
(See Figures 1-1 and 1-2.)

2. If the collected communications materials vary depending
   upon which department or division they are from, the company probably looks disorganized to the outsider. We have
   already discussed the impact that a good image has on the
   public's opinion of the company's financial standing, its personnel, its products, and its reliability. Are the public
   relations director, the marketing, advertising, and sales
   managers; the purchasing agent; and the president speaking
   the same language and to a common end? Are the executives communicating with each other?

3. When viewed all together, does the visual output project a
   dynamic, organized company on the way up with all bases
   covered? Or does it make the company look like a gangling
   adolescent, all arms and legs, each going in a different direction? Does the company look like it is having a hard time
   trying to form a cohesive family organization that works as a
   team? Does it look like the executives have confidence in
   their positions on the team?

4. Life is said to begin at forty. The company is about to
   celebrate its fortieth year in business. Does it look it? If so,
   the firm will not attract as many new, young employees as it
   could and should. It will find it difficult to relate to the
   "younger generation." With the buying power of this
   group, every company must relate to it. But until the company's sales stopped growing, the executives did not seem to
   think they had to. Many established companies continue to
   grow (even if at a lesser rate with time) through sheer
   momentum. In the beginning, it is innovation, flexibility,
   and daring that cause success and growth. Once established,
   many companies lose this dynamism and with time are
   preempted by younger, innovative organizations. Do the
   visual materials look old and tired? Inflexible?

5. The corporation has outstripped its one-store success story
   long ago. In fact, it has also outgrown its regional success

Services Corporation of America

Figure 1-1 If the collected communication materials vary depending upon which department or division they come from, the company probably looks disorganized to the outsider. The visual communication material of Services Corporation of America before its identity program presented these problems.

Figure 1-2 After the identity program, SCA Services' communication materials project a dynamic, organized company on the way up with all bases covered. Designer: Selame Design Associates.

story. It is now a national success. But success has not "spoiled" the company; it has not motivated it to change its image. It still looks the same as it did when it was a one-unit operation—like one person is running the store, greeting the customers, and knows every employee. This image could be a plus, but shouldn't the public also know how large the company is? Does the unchanged image meet all the different state sign and zoning codes and highway beautification programs? How can the firm meet all these different demands at prices it can afford? The building is the image. How can it be replaced, should it be replaced, and with what?

6. The company's various divisions are in different fields of retailing. They all *do* look alike and they *do* adhere to one graphic design system as depicted in the Graphic Manual for Corporate Identification, which has acted as the corporate Bible since the program's inception. However, is the graphic control system an exercise in rigidty? Is status quo thinking settling in over management? Is the firm promoting a look of corporate sterility or stagnation instead of corporate synergism and dynamism? Some corporations acquire other companies mainly for the top management of those companies. If the acquired entrepreneurs feel that their creativity or freedom is stifled within the framework of the identification program, there is danger that they will leave or revolt; the merger will have been for nothing.

7. In a group of companies, there are often reasons for continuing the separate images of the constituents. It takes great experience and design skill to create a system for a corporation that develops an organizational corporate discipline that is valuable in the financial world while allowing diversity. Do the communication materials gathered reflect this expertise? (See Figures 1-3 and 1-4.)

Unfortunately, most of these danger signals do not attract attention until long after the danger point has been reached—when they start showing up as financial losses.

Figure 1-3 Belk's Department Stores allowed its various department stores to retain their individual names. This created a company with many different faces and a need for a corporate identity program.

CASE STUDY: GENERAL CINEMA CORPORATION

The appalling visual sameness of our supermarkets, movie theaters, gas stations, banks, discounters, and so on creates restrictive and protective (of the environment) zoning codes and lethargic consumers and employees. This, of course, can create lethargic profits and limited growth both geographically and internally. To avoid these problems and to stand out in the crowd, General Cinema Corporation decided to begin a corporate identity program.

In 1961, spurred by the imminence of their first stock offering and the ambition to become the nation's leading shopping center theater chain, General Cinema started its planning. In an era of "blockbuster" films playing to long lines of young suburbanites in plush, twin-decked cinema palaces, why should this chain care about a well-designed graphic communications system?

"Because all of our four publics do, that's why," pointed out Richard A. Smith, President of the Boston-based company. These four publics, according to Smith, are "our employees, our stockholders, our patrons, and the general public from which we draw our future employees, stockholders, and patrons."

Top management's personal involvement and time was necessary to execute the design program. From this program came the distinctive corporate symbol, which uses the "GCC" initials to form the image of a projector (see Figure 1-5).

Has the time spent on the corporate identity program been well spent? President Smith thinks so. "It has provided us with an excellent visual representation of the company image—professional, efficient, clean cut, high class, and so on. It has been *extremely successful* in terms of cor-

Figure 1-4 The new corporate identity system still allows Belk the retention of the different names, but unites them visually with the design. Designer: Lippincott & Margulies, Inc.

Figure 1-5A This symbol for the General Cinema Corporation, a motion picture firm, uniquely forms a projector with the company's initials. Functional simplicity is always the best solution, and the symbol in this case provides exactly that. It does more than identify; it captures attention. Had all the initials for this theater chain been kept horizontal, possibly locked into some outside shape, it would have been a stationary symbol. The "action" mark was designed to be used in many media. One of the most impressive applications has been on film.

porate public relations and no doubt has assisted in *financial public relations."*

Of course, the stockholder and prospective stockholder are an important part of the continuing success of any firm. One of the major communication tools directed to stockholders is the annual report. If it relates strongly to the corporate identity, it can build corporate confidence one year upon the next. Each year, GCC's annual report has conveyed through graphics the essence of the president's message.

For example, in 1969 General Cinema made enough beverage acquisitions to become the second largest domestic Pepsi-Cola franchised bottler, and this was shown on the cover of the year's report (see Figure 1-6). The 1970 report chronicled the impressive growth of the company over a decade. The 1971 annual report cover "spoke" about the dynamic growth of the chain's building pattern. (See Figure 1-7). The report should not only relate what happened yesterday, it should also project the idea that management has already appraised tomorrow and is prepared to meet it in an organized manner. Each GCC report meets this criterion.

In 1963, GCC had sales of $15,637,000. In 1973, sales had increased to $245,466,000. During that period, GCC's visual image kept pace with their growing stature and importance in the industry; and we cannot help but feel that their visual image helped them keep that pace.

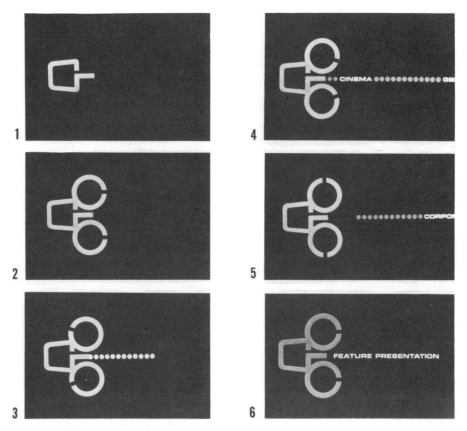

Figure 1-5B   Seen on the large theater screen, the symbol begins to form against a black background. The bright blue of the mark begins to project pink dots to a drum beat followed by the signature in white and then by the main feature title. Designer: Selame Design Associates.

OTHER BENEFITS OF CORPORATE IDENTITY

A corporation can build through its various identity elements. An aura of excellence will capture the imagination of its four publics. A company that looks professional, contemporary, and dynamic induces the best people to seeks positions within that firm. A new corporate identity program is a signal to current and prospective employees, especially the younger ones, that management is not static, is progressive, is not satisfied with yesterday's solutions, and knows that today's problems are different from any other day's problems.

Figure 1-6 Each year, the GCC annual report adds to their equity in their unique corporate identity. The cover is used to visualize the president's yearly message found inside. Its new stature as the second largest domestic Pepsi-Cola franchised bottler was shown on the 1969 report cover, which mingles theater ticket stubs with bottle caps.

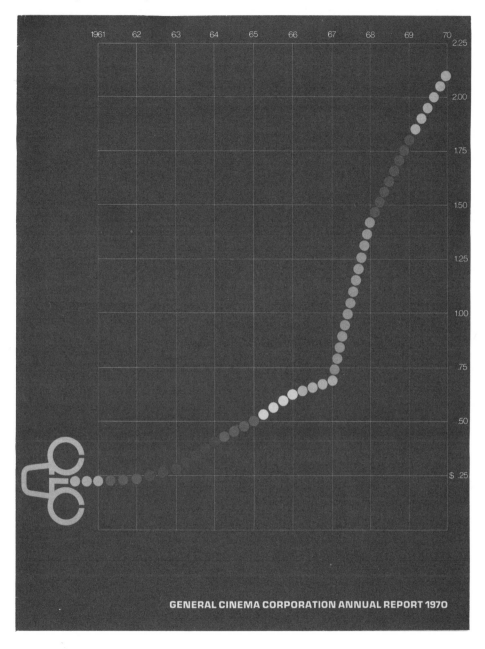

Figure 1-7A The 1970 GCC report cover uses the familiar action symbol to plot the growth of the company over the preceding decade.

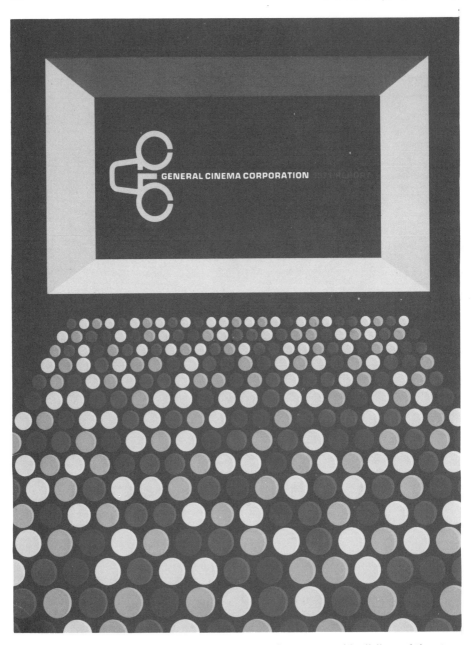

Figure 1-7B   The 1971 GCC report covers the renewed building of theaters by symbolizing the theater screen and audience. GCC report covers designed by Selame Design Associates.

Employee motivation is not just gained by giving out fatter paychecks. Pride in their company, its management, and their work environment rank as high as money motivation. College recruiters often find it difficult to attract young talent to retailing because of the widespread "shopkeeper image." However, this image can be dispelled by corporations who put thought into their identity programs. It is, again, important that the program be an accurate reflection of policies; if it is not, the employees recruited will not stay very long.

Employees moving up the ladder to executive positions want to believe that they are part of a dynamic company that is constantly open to innovation and improvement. Their company's visual identity is a psychological indicator to employees of the company's current position and where it intends to be in the future.

In short, in corporate identification, each element must not only stand successfully alone, but taken as a whole should build a unified story. If the story is interesting and unique, people from each public will listen and want to know more.

chapter 2

Programming the Identity

Not surprisingly, every company that is going through or has gone through a changed identity is usually trying to solve one specific problem. This change usually occurs during or right after a dynamic period of corporate growth, or in order to help trigger a period of dynamic growth. Sometimes, it is too early for a company to embark on a new corporate identity program. If the firm is in a tremendous period of change and the outcome is uncertain, it might be best to wait until the dust clears. If the company is testing new market potentials or beginning to diversify and the final marketing decisions have not been made, it probably would be better to wait, just as it would be if new growth directions that will totally alter the company's image or direction are being considered. Any changes that are imminent, but not clearly defined, dictate a waiting period.

WHO GETS INVOLVED

However, when it is time, how do you know and how do you start? Who or what is the catalyst that starts management on the way to developing a new corporate identity program usually depends upon the size of the company and the reason it embarks on an identity program. In companies with sales under $100 million, there is a good chance that the catalyst is the president, who is still close enough to every facet of the business to pinpoint the problem and the cure for customer, marketing, financial, or employee communications and image ills.

Other executives might also point out the need for a new corporate identity, especially in larger companies. For example, the innovative marketing director creates new markets. Often, the marketing tools he uses for current merchandising projects will not work in the new markets. It is the marketing director's function to translate the products or services of his company into the means to satisfy human needs. As these needs change within society, so must marketing directions, and he must visually translate this to the consumer.

The creation of new companies and products demands the creation of new identifying names, so in this case, the corporate lawyers would get involved or initiate a new program.

If the product the sales manager represented could be made more saleable, he would most likely be the instigator of the innovations. An astute sales manager will, in cooperation with his sales team, look for the reasons behind the lack of sales or less-than-acceptable sales. As a result, he will be very aware of the conditions that need changing and why, so again he would be the one to speak to in developing a new identity.

If the visual image of a firm is in direct contrast to its verbal image, or at least off target, the public relations director would realize that the identity and image needed changing. As some corporate image is unavoidable, he would find it wise to establish a specific and positive image.

The advertising director could also be the executive to start a new program. A well-worn advertising rule has been, "sell the sizzle and not the steak." However, when everyone ends up raving about the sizzle, the difference in the quality and price of the several steaks becomes important. The promotion, advertising, and image should always be ready to change for this reason. It would be up to the advertising director to start the innovation before the competition's sizzle catches up.

Other executives that might see the need for identity changes could be the controller, the merchandising manager, the real estate director, and the architectural planner.

Cooperation is Essential

Marketing decisions appropriately are made before sales programs are established. In order to reap the full benefit of any program, the executives concerned must get together to discuss all the aspects of the company and to visualize the administration, marketing, and sales as parts of a puzzle that must fit together at the right time for the right picture. Companies that have acquired contemporary visual marketing tools already have the advantage of public acceptance and a controlled communications system. These companies have flexibility—they can fit a new product into the total picture. Thus, with an organized marketing setup, more attention can be given to sales.

Firms that have no controlled identity system and are not publicly known usually put forth great effort on a new product with very little return. This would be a time for the marketing and sales managers to think creatively. Do we have a corporate umbrella that fits over this new product or division? Have our packaging and labels been detriments or aids in the corporation's sales? Are we considering all the marketing aids and possibilities, or are we just following the familiar pattern?

No matter who initiates the first thoughts on beginning a new identity program, the chief executive must be in on the planning from the beginning. All executives of the company should also be included. Their feedback and ideas are invaluable—they are the experts in their part of the company, and they would therefore be most qualified to speak on those areas. Their cooperation in initiating the program is essential to its success, and in turn the enthusiasm with which they instill their employees is also essential to the success of the plan at all levels of the company.

In order for a corporate identity program to work well throughout the total company, it would be advisable to take all key employees into the circle of corporate identity knowledge to make sure they understand the long-range assets inherent in a properly coordinated program. They should also understand that success cannot be achieved without their help. Before pencil is put to paper, this communication between top, middle, and first-line management is essential. It is the only way that everyone can agree on, and therefore be enthusiastic about, the final direction to be taken.

INITIATING THE PROGRAM

When senior executives concern themselves with their company's identity, they begin to see objectives and goals in more clearly defined terms. The need for self-analysis brings many well-hidden goals to the surface, causes some goals to be dropped, and others to be reconfirmed. Sometimes, research programs are necessary to aid in this process of defining positive directions and needs.

Study the Problem

First, if a specific, known problem is the reason for a new identity program, verbally define the problem to be resolved. Put it down on paper for reference and for all executives to see. Verbalizing a concise definition will polish any fine points not already honed into final shape.

Once the problem is defined, research available, related data in the industry, such as research projects, statistics, and trade-journal articles. Some of this information could be pertinent to the corporation's specific goals and future directions.[1] Unless there is a specific problem unshared by any other business, it has probably already been researched. Check this out first; the final destination might be reached on someone else's coattails. This will save considerable time and money.

On the other hand, if the problem is peculiar to the corporation or very complex, and the executives would feel more secure if specific research established well-defined directions and needs, several methods could be used. First, an independent research firm could be called in. They would have to be told the questions and problems that need researching in order to be effective. Another method is to retain a design consultant immediately to work with the executives in formulating the research project. The consultant could either research the problem himself, suggest competent specialists to do the research, or hire the researchers himself.

The nature of the research is somewhat defined by the problem itself. For example, if sales have been very good and then drop off, there could be several reasons. Depending upon the time the executives have to spend or the faith they have in the research team, either the management or the researchers would first look into the probable cause of the decline. It could be a gradual change in the population makeup that has just started showing up in sales; it could be a change in the quality of the goods that the firm is receiving; it could be that a new competitor has opened in the same market; or it could be that an existing competitor has changed its policies. The next step, once the general research has been done, is to look into the specifics of the problem and the possible solutions. If the population of the trading area is the problem, the reasearchers would have to go to census reports to find out what the existing breakdown is in terms of age, income brackets, educational achievement, and mobility. Then, checking the data against the store's current policies, the executives could determine that their existing policies are in line with the population's needs and

[1] For information on where to obtain such relevant data, see the Appendix at the end of this book.

wants. If this were the case, then the problem is one of not properly communicating these policies, and the solution is to change the overall look and communications of the company. If the policies are not in line with the needs and wants of a changed population, then this is the problem, and the solution is either to change the policies and then communicate the change, or to go out of business. Of course, not all definitions of problems and then solutions are this easy. It may take a period of from one to three months to define the objectives, the problems, and then to do the proper research into all possible solutions.

When the research is completed, it is then necessary for management, the research consultant, and the design consultant (if one has been called in at this point) to draw from the data the directions, guidelines, and goals for the new corporate identification program. If the research has been done properly, the range of solutions should be self-evident; it is at this point that the specifics are chosen and the general guidelines applicable to the company are chosen and laid out.

Study the Current Communication Materials and Methods

When the project begins, the usual procedure is to appoint someone in the company to be the project director. This person then accumulates letterheads; literature; photographs of buildings, packaging, signs, vehicles, and exhibits; financial statements; contracts; house organs; reports from all branches of the company; and so on.

This material should then be mounted on large boards (20-inch by 30-inch or 30-inch by 40-inch) by category, such as stationery, invoices, legal documents, and so on. Mounting the material in this manner allows ease of handling, ease of making slides for presentation if necessary, and it allows the designers to study the material in an orderly and logical sequence.

Studying this material provides more than a method of getting acquainted with the company's printed output. It often reveals costly and needless duplication. It can also reveal gaps in the material, which means the company has been "making do" with something other than what is proper or good looking, and it can reveal waste, such as using large stationery when a short form would do.

A new company would have little data to collect, but it will probably need all the materials a going enterprise uses in the course of doing business. It is better to plan ahead than make last-minute decisions. This would be the time for a new company to see what is missing and make the design decisions for that material, even if it did not intend to produce that material immediately.

The following checklist covers those materials needed and used by most types of companies. It can be used as a reference to decide which items demand priority. Of course, not all items apply to all types of businesses, and there may be items needed by certain companies not listed here.

Corporate Identification Checklist

1. Stationery
    a. Letterhead, general
    b. Letterhead, executive
    c. Business card, general
    d. Business card, executive
    e. Envelope, #10
    f. Envelope, executive
    g. Envelope, window
    h. Statement
    i. Purchase form
    j. Office memo
    k. Acknowledgment
    l. Shipping papers
    m. News release
    n. Name, phone, address change mailer
    o. Informal, engraved and embossed
    p. Various sizes of Kraft envelopes with logo
    q. Special purposes envelopes
    r. Mailing label
    s. Report form

2. Literature
    a. Annual report
    b. Quarterly report
    c. Capabilities and services brochure
    d. Catalog cover
    e. Catalog pages
    f. New pages for catalog
    g. Public relations information
    h. Sales bulletin
    i. "Literature You Requested"
    j. Newsletter

3. Transportation
    a. Truck cab
    b. Pick-up van
    c. Trailer body
    d. Parking lot decal
    e. Business car
    f. Company aircraft
    g. Ship
    h. Freight and tank car
    i. Materials-handling equipment
4. Packaging
    a. Folding carton
    b. Label
    c. Flexible packaging (bags, sheets, wraps)
    d. Paper bag (carry-out)
    e. Wrapping paper
    f. Plastic container
    g. Plastic bags
    h. Glass container
    i. Can
    j. Tube
    k. Rigid container
    l. Closure
    m. Hang tag
    n. Cloth label
    o. Suit carton
    p. Garment bag
    q. Gift box
    r. Product identification (nameplate)
    s. Shipping containers (crate, corrugated box)
    t. Tape
    u. Decal
    v. Stencil
    w. Stamp
5. Architecture
    a. Exterior design
    b. Interior design
    c. Interior lobby
    d. Interior entrance
    e. Office, showroom, store furnishings, and fixture decor

6. Signs
   a. Exterior (fascia, pylon)
   b. Interior
   c. Directional
   d. Directory
   e. Decals
   f. Remote

7. Marketing/Sales
   a. Sales manual
   b. Uniform
   c. Lapel pin
   d. Audio-visual
   e. Portable exhibits and displays
   f. Permanent exhibits and displays
   g. Window displays
   h. Newspaper advertisements
   i. Television advertisements
   j. Magazines, consumer
   k. Magazines, trade and business
   l. Booklets and brochures
   m. Direct mail
   n. Poster
   o. Merchandising aid
   p. Giveaways
   q. Shopping carts

8. Employee relations
   a. Policy manual
   b. Employee guide
   c. Safety manual
   d. House organ
   e. Nameplate
   f. Identity tag
   g. Five-year pin

9. Dining accessories
   a. Cups (paper, china)
   b. Plates (paper, china)
   c. Napkins (dinner, cocktail; linen, paper)
   d. Matches
   e. Tent card
   f. Menu

g. Ash tray
h. Silverware
i. Glasses
j. Cocktail stirrer
k. Placemat
l. Condiment holders
10. Operational materials
   a. Installment loan book
   b. Savings passbook cover
   c. Trust department portfolio
   d. Check
   e. Withdrawal/deposit slip
   f. Credit card
   g. Gift check
   h. Sales slip

WORKING WITH A DESIGN CONSULTANT

The next step in the program is designing the new materials and the overall look of the new identity. If your company, like CBS or Olivetti, has an art staff noted for excellence of design quality, it is possible to achieve corporate identity on a totally internal basis. However, most firms do not have the need for such specialized design staff skills and must look to the outside for help.

The professional designer gives management a framework to evaluate all their visual image output. It is far better to have someone from the outside establish a corporate identity format and give recommendations and guidelines for future implementations. Unfortunately too many businessmen somehow wind up with amateur designers both inside and outside the firm. A professional designer can actually save a company money through his expertise and advice concerning the production of his client's various visual elements and his ability to speak to different suppliers in their language, thereby eliminating costly mistakes . . . .

A lot of businessmen hesitate to get involved with a designer because they feel he may be inflexible and insensitive to their own ideas. If you and your designer have a good rapport, corporate identity can develop with ease and effectiveness . . . .[2]

---

[2] From an interview with Dr. Martin Annis, President of American Science & Engineering, Cambridge, Massachusetts.

How to Select a Design Consultant

How does a company go about finding a designer with the proper expertise and talents necessary to create totally unified and positive corporate identification programs? Where does the project director look?

There are several professional design organizations who can supply a list of their members, or just of their members in the company's locale.[3] There are often articles noting excellence in design in trade journals, and the research team can look through these pieces for especially admirable design; the design firm's name would also be listed.

If someone in the company is particularly impressed with another company's corporate identity program, determine who did their design work, and then contact the designer. If the firm's advertising agency has a creative staff with a good track record of imaginative and durable corporate identity programs, the project director might want to speak to them. If not, perhaps they could recommend some designers. The public relations consultant might also refer to designers. However, these people often have limited knowledge and skill outside their own field, so their advice should not be taken without a thorough check on the designer in question.

At the outset, the project director could choose several designers from any of these sources and ask them to mail him their credentials and several examples of their work on similar programs. This way, several of the firms will be eliminated immediately, saving them and the project director time. Those firms whose work does not appeal visually or that do not have extensive experience with corporate identity programs should probably be eliminated right away.

An understanding of the design processes involved in corporate identification is a great aid in both choosing and working with the design firm. However, if the project director does not have any background in this field and does not have time to take a crash course, how can he, or any other executive in the company, distinguish between good and bad design, or between those designers that can and cannot execute their ideas? First, *good design is original.* It is also not a matter of prettiness, but one of filling a need. A good designer will make each item on the checklist function as part of a whole. Every component of the system from signage down to menus should work both alone and as part of the whole program, and it should get the message across. Weak design, on the other hand, is a borrower. Tailfins belong on airplanes; the public did not take long to re-

[3] For a list of these organizations, see the Appendix.

ject these useless appendages on automobiles.

If the samples the designer has submitted show good design, and the company is interested in hiring him, check his credentials. Has he had similar experience? Check with the people he has worked for. Was he a good co-worker? If he has had experience, added his ideas and design skill to the ideas and desires of the people he worked with (as opposed to always disagreeing or always agreeing, which is just as dangerous), then chances are he is suitable for the job.

Cost of Identity Design

The fees for a corporate identity design program can range from as low as $500 to well over $200,000, depending upon the experience of the designer, the amount of work involved, and the complexity of the assignment. Usual fees for the usual amount of work range from $7,000 to $30,000 for the first phase of the program, which might be all that is needed.

In some firms, the first phase of the project for the designer, as we have mentioned, is the research study. This fee could range from $1,000 to over $20,000, again depending upon the designer and the amount of study needed. The study could be as simple as a statement after a month's consultation that the designer suggests that the company follows through with the identity program.

Most experienced and/or creative consultants capable of guiding a firm toward total corporate identity are to be found in the offices of industrial and graphic designers. Most of these firms will become involved in the architectural design, interior design, advertising design, package and product design, sales promotion, exhibits, and so on, or will consult with others who do specialize in those fields. Their fees, which fall into the range already stated, depend on the geographical location as well as the other factors mentioned.

In almost no case does the new design cost more than the company would ordinarily spend in equipment renewal and maintenance. In fact, adhering to the new program guidelines often streamlines operations by causing simpler, more uniform procedures, and so frequently lowers operating costs. Of course, the less complicated and involved a corporate identity program is, the less expensive it will be. The larger the number of executives who must be pleased by the design, the higher the fee. The more visual areas covered by the design project, the more applications necessary, the more complex the firm's visual communications system, the higher the fee will go.

The Designer's Responsibilities

We have already mentioned that the designer will sometimes do the necessary research for the project, and that he must work closely with the executives involved in all phases of the project. The necessary applications can be determined from the shape of the company's current identity, the problem involved, and the corporate identification checklist.

The designer also often develops the graphic manual, which then becomes the guideline for all future visual projects at every level of the firm. It would be used by anyone in the company who has the responsibility for ordering or using any visual material, from trucks to signs to advertising to placemats. Sometimes, the visual changes need testing before being implemented on a permanent basis and before the final manual is drawn up. In this case, the designer is often asked to make himself available to division and store managers to answer specific questions and make on-the-spot decisions. If this is not one of his responsibilities, it then would fall to the project director.

The designer and any assistants he might have will need the right answers at the right time from the right people. The president, of course, is the final decision maker, but often it is the executives responsible for the various areas of the company that work daily with the designer. The initial meetings will often be the only time when the designer works directly with the chief executive, and that is why it is so important that his opinions and impressions be carefully noted then. However, unless he delegates all responsibility for the program to someone else, it is very important that the designer knows at all times that he is working with the president's approval.

More and more, corporate design systems serve as the organizational medium for the tremendous quantity of visual communications issued by the business community. The graphic designer will be called upon more frequently at the higher management level, not to design a particular brochure or letterhead, but to involve himself with design in total communications. This, in turn, will demand of the designer that he be oblivious to fads and fashion, and sure of design in the classic sense—structure, discipline, simplicity.

Most important, the end result is only as good and as satisfying to the company as the direction the designer is given. Without total cooperation and good communication, the time of everyone involved will be wasted.

chapter 3

Trademarks

INTRODUCTION

When man traded face to face, there was no need for a trademark to identify the source of the goods. The producer's face was his trademark. The satisfied purchaser simply returned to the same person in the same stall in the same marketplace to again purchase the same article. However, once the trader's success and reputation spread outside his immediate area, he needed a mark to distinguish his product from others.

The use of trademarks dates from the times of our very earliest recorded history. In ancient Egypt, bricks carried the manufacturer's name and were often also identified by intricate pictures. Nebuchadnezzar had his name stamped on every brick of his palace. Five thousand years ago, Chinese pottery carried marks on the bases to signify the origin of the product. The ancient Hindustanis and Greeks followed a similar practice. During the reign of King Solomon, the Phoenician quarry mechanics who prepared the stone for construction projects painted unique signs of origin on the blocks in vermillion paint to prove their claim to wages. Trademarks from the age of the Roman Empire have been found on lead pipe, marble, glassware, bronze instruments, gold and silverware, and even the bread of

Pompeii, which was stamped with the maker's seal. Wherever commerce was brisk and competitive, trademarks were used to identify products or establishments.

Until the Industrial Revolution, trademarks played a limited but important role. As early as the Middle Ages, large quantities of guild and municipal legislation began regulating the use of marks. Much of modern trademark law and many common-law rules concerning trademarks are surprisingly similar to this legislation.

The trademark as an instrument of modern marketing communication came into general use in the early 1900s. Today, there are about 400,000 interstate trademarks registered in the U.S. Patent Office, and this number grows by about 20,000 registrations a year.[1] These figures do not include the thousands of *intra*state trademarks registered in the fifty states. Trademark registration is also possible in over 150 countries around the world. These numbers show how important the trademark has become; in fact, many consider it to be the most valuable asset of their businesses.

BASIC FACTS ABOUT TRADEMARKS[2]

Definition

A *trademark* is a word, name, symbol, or device, or any combination of these, used by a merchant or manufacturer to identify his goods and distinguish them from those of his competitors. A trademark is the same thing as brand name. This is not to be confused with a *trade name*, which identifies the business, not the product.

Functions

The primary function of a trademark is that stated in the definition: to distinguish one person's goods from another's. However, a trademark also serves as an indication to consumers that the quality of the goods bearing the mark remains constant. It also serves as the focal point of advertising to create and maintain a demand for the product.

Ownership

A trademark may be owned (and may be registered) by an in-

[1] United States Patent Office.

[2] We are indebted to Dorothy Fey and the United States Trademark Association for much of the information contained in the balance of this chapter.

TERMINOLOGY AND ITS ORIGIN

House Mark—House Colors

At the time of the Napoleonic Wars, pilgrims and travelers had become an enormous industry in England and on the Continent. Innkeepers identified their houses with religious and heraldic symbols. (Beer and ale were brewed in monasteries, and each house was noted for its particular type of beverage.) Some displayed a coat of arms to boast of royal affiliations. Guild members identified their wares with monograms and marks.

Coutts Bank

One of the oldest banking institutions in London, The House of Coutts (1692) used a house mark of three crowns for its identity. It is in use to this day.

Registered Trademark

With the Industrial Revolution came increased rivalry and often plagiarism. Owners of identifying devices sought binding protection through patents and legal proof of ownership. Heated court battles created new laws and rulings, and the registered trademark became a protectable means of identification.

Logotype or Sig Cut

During the mid 1900s, the repetitive use of trademarks forced letterpress printers to stock drawers full of trademark plates, or signature cuts, in every conceivable size. These were sometimes referred to as logotypes, and soon the word "logo" became synonymous with "trademark."

33

dividual, a firm, a partnership, a corporation, or an association or other collective group.

Types of Trademarks

There are four types of marks that can be registered with the U.S. Patent Office: (1) trademarks that identify products; (2) service marks that are used in the sale or advertising of services to distinguish them from the services of others, including some radio or television program titles and slogans; (3) collective marks used by members of cooperatives, associations, or other collective groups to identify and distinguish the group's products from those of others; and (4) certification marks that show that the products have been certified as to quality, method of manufacture, materials, and so on by a certain person, business, or group.

SELECTING A TRADEMARK

It is becoming more and more difficult for businesses to select a trademark that is informative, distinctive, appealing to the public, and that is adaptable to a total identity program. The corporate symbol that is used for your program may or may not be the same as your product's trademark. However, if the firm is new, why not choose one for both functions? It will be a tremendous help to advertising and customer recall and will cut the selection process in half.

Using an Existing Trademark

If the firm currently uses a certain trademark for existing products, this mark can often be used on new products. If the current trademark has good recognition and is thought of highly by the public, then using it on new products will help sell them. An existing mark can also be slightly modified and extended to cover a whole family of products. For example, the world-famous "Kodak," which was originally a name for cameras, has been extended to "Kodachrome," "Kodacolor," and so on to their other products, and affords instant recognition of the producer of these goods.

Finding a New Trademark

If the firm has no appropriate existing trademark for a new product, or has no trademark at all, there are three types of marks from which to choose. There are four guidelines to keep in mind while looking for a new mark: (1) it should be easy to remember and pronounce; (2) it should be pleasing to the eye and ear; (3) it should have no unfavorable connotations in English or in the language of any foreign country where the firm is planning to build or now has branches; and (4) it should lend itself to visualization, be adaptable to any advertising or visual medium, and lend itself to the design of the total identity program.

With these requirements in mind, the company can look at the three types of marks. The first type is *meaningless or arbitrary words* that are coined for the express purpose of use as the trademark (meaningless) or are picked at random from the dictionary and have no relation to the product (arbitrary). For instance, "Kodak" was chosen by George Eastman after he had tried many arbitrary letter combinations. He also liked the sound of the letter *k*. Shell Oil Company got its name from the family's background; Marcus Samuel began selling the shells his children collected, and the business evolved into an international trade in Oriental curios, copra, and eventually kerosene and oil. Arbitrary trademarks can also be numbers, initials, historical or mythological character names, or picture-word marks, such as "White Owl."

As designers, we feel that the use of picture-words can be confusing to the public unless they are carefully chosen and designed. For example, many companies use Indians or crowns as part of their picture-words. Each is designed differently and each is a registered, protectable trademark. However, they can be confusing to the public, who might remember only the crown and not its design or the company's name. For this reason, we try for uniqueness by forming the picture out of the initials of the company; for example, the Goodwill Industries' smiling face that was formed from the initial G.

The second type of mark that may be chosen is the *suggestive* mark. Some businessmen feel it is more appealing and easier to introduce to the public because they are already familiar with the word in the mark. This type is not descriptive of the product, and therefore is almost as easy to protect as the meaningless mark. It describes a connotation that the producer would like to associate with his product. For example, "Halo" shampoo connotes soft highlights around the crown of the hair.

The third type of mark is *descriptive* and is the most difficult to protect. This type either describes the product, is the name of the owner, or is the name of the place where the product is made. In order to protect such a trademark, the producer must create a second meaning in the minds of the public and other producers of the same type of product. If this second meaning is not acquired, the mark might not qualify for registration. One way to protect a descriptive trademark is to employ a unique design. Kennedy, a very common last name, is not protectable. However, by using the name as a distinctive signature, they have been able to protect their trademark.

REGISTERING THE TRADEMARK

Once the trademark considered best for the product has been selected, the firm must determine if it is available for use. The mark must not be a duplicate of any existing mark and must not be confusingly similar. A search must be conducted to be sure the selected trademark is clear. Once this is ascertained, and the mark has been used, an application for registration can be made.

The U.S. Patent Office has jurisdiction over all federal trademark registrations. If the goods or services that bear the mark are sold or shipped in interstate commerce, then the trademark may be registered at the federal level. If they are involved in intrastate commerce only, then the mark may be registered in the state where the goods or services are sold. If the firm is involved in international commerce, then the trademark may be registered in each trading country.

Again, registering a trade *name* should not be confused with trademark registration. For instance, "The Eastman Kodak Company" is the trade name and cannot be registered. However, the "Kodak" worked into the seal is the trademark and can be (and is) registered. At present, no provision is made in the federal trademark law to register trade names.

Qualifications

To qualify for registration, the trademark must be available and must be *in use* at the time the application is submitted. The person or company applying for a registration must show the date of first use and show samples of the mark as it is actually being used—that is, attached to the product. A similar procedure is necessary for registration in any state.

Advantages of Registration

It is not necessary to apply for trademark registration in any given time period after its first use. In fact, a trademark is afforded some protection at common law through its use and so does not have to be registered at all. If the firm can show that the mark meets standards of registrability, that it used the mark before another firm did, and that the other firm's mark is the same or confusingly similar, then it may have a case against any infringer.

However, if the mark is registered, these matters of proof are made much simpler. There are four basic advantages to registering a mark:

1. It gives notice of the firm's claim to the mark.
2. It creates presumptions of ownership and the exclusive right to use the mark.
3. It may eventually represent conclusive evidence of the right to exclusive use; for example, in a lawsuit.
4. It may be necessary or helpful in obtaining registration in some foreign countries.

Notice of Registration

There are three ways to designate that a trademark is registered and the property of the firm.

1. "Registered in U.S. Patent Office"
2. "Reg. U.S. Pat. Off."
3. "®"

It is advisable to have this notice following or near the trademark itself.

It is illegal to use such notices until the trademark has been registered. However, until the registration is complete, a notation such as "Trademark," "Brand," or "TM" may be used. This serves as a notice that the firm does intend to register the mark or that it does consider the mark its property under common law.

Duration of Registration

As long as a company does wish to retain its registration, it can do so. A trademark registration is good for twenty years, and then can be renewed every twenty years after perpetually, provided that the trademark continues to be in use.

TRADEMARKS MAY BE LOST

If the company's trademark becomes misused by the public as the name of the product, that is, as a common descriptive word, the firm may have a problem. The trademark may become available for use by competitors in a similar manner if the mark is successfully challenged as generic and the registration cancelled. This has happened to many large and well-informed companies. In 1921, Bayer lost its exclusive right in the United States to the name "aspirin," and in 1936 Dupont's "cellophane" became common property. In 1963, King-Seely lost its exclusive use of the word *thermos*, other than the exclusive right to use a capital *T*.

A mark may become generic due to its misuse by the firm's executives or employees. This is more likely to happen to a descriptive mark, and is the primary danger in choosing a descriptive word as a trademark. To help prevent the mark from becoming generic, it should not be used as a possesive, in the plural, as a descriptive word, or as a verb. Using it in any of these forms not only alters the way in which the mark is registered, but it also changes it in the minds of the public into a common, descriptive word. When this happens, an eager competitor can challenge the firm's right to its exclusive use.

Therefore, employees and even the press should be instructed on the mark's proper use, and their use of the mark should be checked carefully at all times. It is especially important that advertisements carry the mark only in its proper form. This will help drive home that form in the minds of the public and help prevent their alteration of the mark into a common, or generic, word.

SUMMARY

In a company's infancy, it is sometimes difficult to predict in what direction and how much the company will grow. It is therefore very difficult to predict where a trademark will be used and which mark to use. However, due to the value of the trademark, it is worth the time and effort to choose a mark that will stand the test of time and place and resist the danger of falling into generic use.

Many firms do not realize the value of a trademark until the patents on their products run out and all they have left are their trademarks. The mark continues to distinguish their product from those of competitors, even when those competitors are taking advantage of the patent's expiration and duplicating the product. The trademark should therefore be treated with respect and tender loving care.

So, even if the firm has found that great name that is easy to remember, read, and speak, has no unpleasant connotations, can be adapted to all visual media, and is unique, there are still many legalities that should be considered carefully. We have covered these aspects in general, but in a book of this nature it is impossible to cover the legal details.

For more information, write to the U.S. Patent Office for the pamphlet entitled, "General Information Concerning Trademarks." For more detailed information, write the Superintendent of Documents, Washington, D.C. 20402, for a copy of the "Trademark Rules of Practice of the Patent Office with Forms and Statutes." The first pamphlet is less than one dollar, and the second costs around three dollars. A complete list of publications regarding specific areas of trademark concerns can be obtained from the U.S. Trademark Association, 6 East 45th Street, New York, N.Y. 10017.

chapter 4

The Corporate Symbol

IMPORTANCE OF THE SYMBOL

The Pharoahs knew it, David knew it, Christ's disciples knew it, kings and queens have known it: a symbol can be the most powerful motivating tool known to man. Although symbols have always been created and used by people to communicate with other people, only a few graphic symbols have been accepted into common usage. Perhaps this is because most symbols tend to confuse the viewer rather than communicate in the simplest visual terms.

Because the corporate symbol is the central, unifying factor of the identity program, it must be clear, not confusing. It must say something about who the company is or what the purpose of the company is in a form that can be seen and comprehended quickly, and then remembered easily.

Just as it is easier to remember a person's face than his name, so it should be easier to remember a company's symbol than its name. The identity program ultimately relies on the symbol for its strength. If the symbol is weak, confusing, hard to remember or decipher, or badly proportioned, it can have an adverse effect on the entire program. The symbol must be, at the very least, functional: distinctive, simple, and easy to remember. If, in addition, it is meaningful (tells a story) and is a delight to the eye, it will give the whole program a tremendous boost.

CHOOSING THE SYMBOL

A symbol (like a trademark), although visualized by the designer, is chosen by the company's executives. The symbol can take one of five basic forms and can be expressed in as many ways as there are colors, typefaces, and shapes. What are the factors to consider in making such an important decision? What design considerations need to be taken into account? Even if the firm decides to use its trademark for the corporate symbol, it still has decisions to make. Should it be identical to the trademark, or should it be stylized in some way? As each of the three types of trademarks (meaningless, suggestive, or descriptive) can take any of the five forms, should the trademark take one form and the symbol another? Should a slight addition to or subtraction from the trademark be made before it is used as the symbol?

Of course, underlying all symbol decisions will be the decision maker's personal likes, dislikes, and opinions concerning aesthetic considerations and image. Also influential in the final decision are the company's areas of visual exposure, the market segment to be reached, and the budget set aside for reproducing the symbol, as some are naturally more complicated and expensive to reproduce than others.

The ability and creativity the designer brings into its visualization will also affect the symbol's outcome. Again, when the designer is familiar with the various "faces" of the company and knows what is in the minds of the executives, he can do a more satisfying job. The more sensitive the designer and the more he knows about the company, the better the chance that he will come up with the essence of the company in a simple yet meaningful symbol.

The Seal

The first of the five basic forms of corporate symbols is the *seal*, which is a name or group of words worked into one total form (see Figure 4-1). This might be the choice of a service company as it might be difficult to depict their business in a mark. It would also be the choice of a firm that wanted to use its name or motto for its symbol, but wanted it used against a background that gave the letters depth and warmth.

The Monoseal

The second type of symbol is the *monoseal*, which is made up of initials that are worked into a form like the seal (see Figure 4-2). This has the same advantages as the monogram, but also has the added benefits afforded by the seal's background. Putting a monogram into a seal can add "warmth" to the initials, thereby satisfying those who feel that initials alone are too sterile.

The Monogram

The *monogram* symbol is comprised of initials used in a unique manner (see Figure 4-3). Initials can be taken in by the viewer as quickly as a mark, and so would be ideal for a company widely known by its initials. Initials can also be read by people in any country using the same alphabet. Some people feel initials are too sterile, depersonalized, and very forgettable. This would be true only for companies not known by their initials or not often exposed to the public's eye, such as manufacturers. For others, however, such as IBM or RCA, initials are worth a thousand words or pictures.

The Signature

A *signature* is a name or group of words rendered in a particular consistent style (see Figure 4-4). Some executives and designers feel that this symbol is the best identification for a company, just as a person's name is his best identification. These people feel that the name is more personal and distinctive than a picture or seal. This symbol would not be practical for highly diversified companies whose separate parts use different names unless united by a common typestyle.

The Mark

The last of the five basic forms is the *mark*. This is an abstract or pictorial graphic device. The *abstract mark* is a shape or device that is usually geometrical (see Figure 4-5). It may or may not express a general feeling (masculine, feminine, technological, organic, and so on), but it is not pictorial or typographic. It has no visual connection with a company's products, services, or name, other than that relationship established through promotional effort. If the mark tells a story, it is called a *glyph* (see Figure 4-6). A glyph is comprised of simple graphic lines and tells a visual story about the company's name, major product line, or area of business

Figure 4-1   The Seal: A name or group of words rendered in a cohesive form. Designers: New York Life, Lippincott & Margulies, Inc.; Blue Seal, Selame Design Associates; Kodak, Kodak Staff; Ford, Ford Staff.

Figure 4-2   The Monoseal: A monogram or initial within a shape or seal-like form. Designers: Maytag, Dave Chapman, Goldsmith & Yamasaki, Inc.; Westinghouse, Paul Rand; PPG, Lippincott & Margulies, Inc.; General Electric, GE Staff.

Figure 4-3   The Monogram: A letter or combination of letters rendered in a distinctive manner devoid of confinement. Designers: IBM, Paul Rand; AVX Aerovox and E-Z Shops, Selame Design Associates; RCA, Lippincott & Margulies, Inc.

Figure 4-4   The Signature: A company name rendered in a particular and consistent manner. Designers: Eaton, Lippincott & Margulies, Inc.; Hemingway Transport and Ludlow, Selame Design Associates.

Figure 4-5   The Abstract: A graphic device, geometric or otherwise, that represents a company or service. Designers: Atlantic Richfield, Carol Lipper & Tomoko Miho; North American Rockwell, Saul Bass & Associates; Exolon, Selame Design Associates; Chrysler, Lippincott & Margulies, Inc.

Figure 4-6   The Glyph: A mark that pictorializes a company's service or area of competence. Designers: United Fund, Saul Bass & Associates; Woolmark, Francesco Saroglia; American Telephone and Telegraph, Saul Bass & Associates; CBS, William Golden.

Figure 4-7   The Alphaglyph: A mark formed around a letter or letters that pictorializes a company's service or area of competence. Designers: Foreign Autopart, Selame Design Associates; International Paper, Lester Beall; General Cinema, Mutual Oil, and Goodwill Industries, Selame Design Associates.

concern. Once learned, the glyph is easy to recall, it can be taken in quickly by the eye as there is nothing to read, and because it involves no words the glyph can be understood by speakers of any language. For these reasons, the glyph is especially good for companies with foreign branches or for highway signage. If the simple graphic lines used to tell the glyph's story are partially comprised of an initial, the mark is called an *alphaglyph* (see Figure 4-7). The alphaglyph's initial provides a quick clue to the company's name, and the pictograph tells an immediate story.

The Combination Symbol

Figure 4-8 depicts a *combination symbol*, which is comprised of a mark and signature. This can stand as the company's symbol, or it can be devised so that at times either the mark or the signature is used alone. The parts of this symbol should be related in proportion and style, and both elements should be strong enough to stand alone when necessary.

Figure 4-8   The combination symbol is formed from a mark and a signature. In the Mutual Oil Company, an independent gasoline station chain, their "M" depicts two figures tipping their caps, signalling service. The "M" and caps are red; the dots (heads) are orange. The service attendants wear red uniforms to unify the image. Designer: Selame Design Associates.

An added benefit of the combination symbol, especially when used as a trademark as well, is that it is legally protectable, no matter how generic the name. For example, "Foreign Auto Parts" is much too generic to protect. However, when put into a combination symbol, it can be protected. Figure 4-9 shows the company's symbols before and after the identity program. The mark in the new symbol depicts a stylized car, but is also made up of two letter *f*'s, that together also form a letter *A*, therefore using both of the company's initials. With a slight name change, making "auto parts" one word and dropping the *s*, the symbol becomes clean of extra lines, distinctive, and easy to remember.

Figure 4-9 Because their name was too generic and their seal lacked distinction, Foreign Autopart had the symbol redesigned. The new combination symbol, at right, shows their symbol comprised of two "f's," which then form an "A." Designer: Selame Design Associates.

Which Symbol is Best?

There are advantages and disadvantages to using each of the five forms. The personal opinions of the people choosing the symbol and planning the program have the heaviest bearing on which is chosen and why.

In general, the combination symbol is most useful for unlimited applications. However, both businessmen and designers have strong opinions about which symbol they prefer. Some do not like the combination symbol because it still involves reading words, rather than just looking at a simple picture. For this reason, the followers of this school of thought believe that a descriptive mark or glyph is most effective and they cannot see the reasoning behind using any other symbol. There are good designers who argue that initials are quite valid and useful, and there are equally good designers who condemn "alphabet soup" symbols. Many people like the simplicity of abstract marks. They feel that the designs are simple, easy to remember, do not pin down the business of the company, and so can be used in the future when the company diversifies. However, some people also feel that abstract marks are meaningless graphic excercises. Instead of stimulating, they feel these abstractions sterilize. They also feel that the abstract mark seems to have a hidden meaning that is known to no one and can be deciphered by no one, and is therefore forgotten as soon as it is out of the viewer's sight. We feel that the types of marks that allow instant recognition, such as glyphs, are especially advantageous symbols for companies that are now, or that are planning to go, international.

No matter which is chosen or why, well-conceived and well-designed symbols all have something in common. They manage to be distinctive but economical. They convey the name and/or the purpose of the company or an image that the company wants to project with the fewest possible graphic lines.

Figure 4-10   A contrast in symbols: The old symbols appearing at the left lacked dignity and clarity; the improved new forms at right also eliminate reproduction problems when reduced or used on surfaces other than paper. Designer: Selame Design Associates.

DESIGN CONSIDERATIONS IN CHOOSING A SYMBOL

Any present or future uses of the symbol have to be taken into consideration from a design viewpoint. First of all, the design has to be clean enough (free of superfluous lines) to reproduce well on all surfaces: metal, glass, paper, polyethylene, and so on. Because all these surfaces

THE EVOLUTION OF A SYMBOL

Many times, what was meant to be the "official seal" becomes the company's "symbol."

1889   1900

After being asked by printers, companies embark upon a "clean-up" campaign in order to make the old seal easier to reproduce and remember. The owner of the seal often feels that the original has to stay intact to as great an extent as possible. The result is therefore a symbol-seal; neither a symbol in the true sense nor an original seal.

Besides lacking in signal value, some seals have graphic limitations and are especially prone to poor reproduction qualities. Platemakers and printers refer to these reduced seals as "bugs," due to their resemblance to insects when greatly reduced and when the type fills in.

1921   1939

During the past two decades, and into this one, the newer marks have taken on a more sophisticated graphic simplicity. They are designed to be identified instantly in an ever-increasing jungle of ads, signing, and competitive attention-getting devices. If the mark is a simple pictograph, such as Bell's newest symbol, it is easy to recognize and understand in all countries, and is called a glyph.

1964   1969

Symbols reprinted by permission of AT&T.

have different qualities and because the processes involved in working the symbol on these surfaces differ, the design has to be flexible in this respect (see Figure 4-10).

Another important design requirement is that the design must reproduce well in different sizes. If it is as effective at a quarter of an inch on a business card as it is at twenty feet high on a store front, it has good potential. Unless a symbol can be reduced and still retain strong recognition and unless it can be enlarged and not become an aesthetic outrage, it does not serve its intended purpose as a quick and visually pleasing identifier.

A third design test is how the symbol looks when it is endlessly repeated, such as on can after can on a store shelf. If it becomes boring or annoying, the symbol in question is not a good choice. A good symbol also works well in color and black and white. It must also be strong enough to stand out in an advertisement; a newspaper page when viewed as a whole is a blur of lines, tones, and type. If the symbol becomes a part of the blur, its purpose is lost.

For high retention value, geometric forms are preferable to illustrations because there are fewer lines for the eye to take in. Especially under today's varied and sometimes difficult viewing conditions, the less the eye has to see, the more the viewer can remember. Complicated illustrative symbols do not work well in short exposure, poor lighting, or competitive surroundings.

Case Study: Howard Johnson's[1]

Howard D. Johnson always used total merchandising concepts to market his merchandise. In 1931, sophisticated corporate identification programs were not the consideration of most entrepreneurs. Yet, intuitive good merchandising techniques are usually part of all successful operations dealing with the public, and so it was with Howard Johnson. With an inspiration worthy of Barnum, Johnson began to paint the roofs of his establishments a bright orange to attract passing motorists.

In 1938, he called in a young Boston designer, John Alcott. Johnson had a big black van and wanted to know what Alcott could do to make it look attractive. The two men both felt that everything associated with a company identified that company, including such peripheral matters as the

---

[1] The information in this case study is from an interview with John Alcott of Westwood, Massachusetts.

company's trucks. Alcott visited the firm before redesigning the van. He was searching for one element that could tie all aspects of the company together. At that time, the restaurant chain sold and packaged only a few products. The Simple Simon fable illustration was used on some of the packages. The designer saw that illustration as a symbol of playful, recreational dining and felt that it was also universally known. He refined the sketch, designed it to be an integral element of the firm's identity, and used it on all items related to the company. (See Figure 4-11.) He became the chain's design consultant for the next thirty years.

Figure 4-11 The original Howard Johnson's symbol. Designer: John Alcott.

Figure 4-12 The new Howard Johnson's symbol. Designer: Gianninoto Associates, Inc.

In 1954, Alcott became consulting Art Director for the firm. Both Alcott and Johnson took corporate colors seriously. Instead of the usual, less accurate method of specifying color by "match the last run," Howard Johnson's standarized their orange and blue. Even tolerances in incandescent, fluorescent, and natural lighting were considered and allowances in tone and depth were established for these differences.

The three most important graphic elements familiar to the public were the roof design and the orange and turquoise colors. Shrewd as it was about roof painting, the company didn't recognize its roof as a ready-made symbol until very recently. In 1965, the research firm of Daniel Yankelovich discovered it was one of the best identifications ever developed. Out went the 35-year-old Simple Simon and the Pieman symbol. In came the stylized silhouette of the orange rooftop and spire (see Figure 4-12). This symbol is being tested on some on-site pylon signage with the letters *H.J.* This is being done, according to Group Vice President,

Marketing, Frank Lionette, in order to increase the highway viewing distance. Where local codes restrict the size of the signs, a bolder statement can be made with the orange roof and initials than with the entire signature. The company therefore feels the variation in its trademark is justified in these cases.

Case Study: The Stop and Shop Companies

Over a period of eight years in the 1960s, an unusual corporate identity system enabled The Stop & Shop Companies to pass on the glyphic genes of their corporation and established divisions to their younger additions. The Stop & Shop Companies felt that as the prestige of the parent company grew, the subsidiaries would benefit, and *vice versa*.

This program has an underlying visual thread of family relationships. Their various retail divisions are related visually by the same simplicity of circle and line, yet each symbol tells its own unique story and function.

The supermarket symbol, shown in Figure 4-13A, says: We are members of The Stop & Shop Companies. The management would like the customer to stop for a while, come into our store, and make a purchase (stoplights). This is a self-service store (shopping cart). We are part of a larger company and are proud of this (symbol relationship to corporate whole). We use this mark as an acknowledgment that a proud organization stands behind its products.

The drugstore chain symbol (see Figure 4-13B) says: We are members of the Stop & Shop Companies (three discs relate to stoplights in supermarket symbol and to corporate symbol). We dispense drug products and have a pharmaceutical department (pills and mortar and pestle). We are part of a larger company and are proud of this (symbol relationship to whole). We use this mark on our private label products to show that they are quality controlled and we are proud to stand behind them.

The Stop & Shop identity program was a top-to-bottom campaign. In some of their supermarkets, the symbol appears even on the handles of the shopping carts. The symbol is easy to remember, affords quick recognition, and cuts across language barriers. The program has been continually checked for efficacy and has been modernized as the years passed. They have now simplified the symbol even more by eliminating one circle.

Figure 4-13A Designer: Selame
Design Associates.

Figure 4-13B Designer: Selame
Design Associates.

CHANGING A KNOWN SYMBOL

Many executives hesitate to change their company's present symbol because they feel they will loose their already known identity. There is the possibility that changing a symbol will dissatisfy some customers, but if the overall program is successful, the gains will outweigh the losses. If the company is really reluctant to change its symbol, even though the sales figures indicate that a change is necessary, making a gradual change might be a satisfactory compromise.

Case Study: Bloomingdale's

The familiar Bloomingdale's old-era script signature gave way to a contemporary, understated lower-case signature (see Figure 4-14). It appeared on all Bloomingdale's print material and on new exterior signage.

Of course, it is impossible to please everyone when you change your symbol, as the following letter indicates:

Bloomingdale's old sig was unique, distinctive.

To the Editor: Your issue of Jan. 15 has an article by Lorraine Baltera ("Retail Marketing") which talks about the changes at Bloomingdale's. I note with sadness that they have replaced what I consider a distinctive and unique signature (which Lorraine calls a "scribble") with a bit of fancy-schmancy, and illegible, lettering (which Lorraine has labeled "sleek"). I can't help remembering the John Wanamaker signature which had so much class and could not be aped by anyone. A scribble and unsleek it may have been. But I believed what J. W. signed, as I believe what Alfred Knopf, the publisher, signs—and for the same reasons. Behind each signature was a man, or the representation of a man. But behind the "sleek letering" is an art director looking at his hand mirror.[2]

Figure 4-14   The old (top) and new Bloomingdale's signatures. The new symbol is easier to read and is more contemporary. Designer: Massimo Vignelli.

However, consideration must be given to the greatest marketing potential, even though a small number of your customers might resist change.

Case Study: Brigham's

Originally a regional New England chain, Brigham's is now part of the Jewel Companies of Chicago. The restaurant company decided in 1964 that it was time to aim for the young family market and build up sales

---

[2] *Advertising Age* (January, 1973), from "Letters to the Editor."

of its light food and private-label grocery items. Originally, it was one store with two identities: one for ice cream and candy, one for baked goods. Unity and one retail name was the goal.

Until that time, the chain was identified by an Old English letter style that was not easy to read, especially on their signs. They had Selame Design modernize and unify the two signatures, "Brigham's" and "Dorothy Muriel." At that time, they were not ready to go further. Management felt that a major revamping design program was necessary, but knew they had tremendous equity in their well-established New England image; so, they did not want to make the change all at once. The solution was to design an identity that was familiar to the established market and yet also appeal to the younger generation.

A blue signature, contemporary and easy to read, enclosed in an oval, was designed and hand-lettered for Brigham's and Dorothy Muriel. Whenever two colors were used in signing, a bright red dot appeared over Brigham's *i*. This was not a full solution but a transitional plan. Happily, it

Figure 4-15 The original Old English lettering of Brigham's signature was replaced in 1960 by the script, which was modernized and brightened up. Designer: Selame Design Associates.

was one that could be built upon. For five years, the signatures were used on signing, packaging, and advertising. In that period, the image of a staid, older ice cream chain was discarded completely, and the public happily accepted the new Brigham's. (See Figure 4-15.)

Figure 4-16 This adaptation of the basic Brigham's signature proved especially useful for packaging and decoration. Designer: Selame Design Associates.

It was now ready for the missing part of its corporate structure— a mark. The designers created a festive, fun-looking mark. The five-petal mark has four blue petals and one magenta to spark curiosity, make it more visually exciting, and to protect it legally. (See Figure 4-16.)

SUMMARY

Although the major element in the corporate identity program, the symbol is often the least-planned factor. Unplanned, it can undermine the whole identity program. Rigid design considerations are important, but planned flexibility is also important. This flexibility will be necessary to carry the symbol through the graphic processes necessary to applying it in different sizes and on different surfaces and to carry it over the years. Symbols should not be regarded as static and untouchable, especially if their usefulness or effectiveness has passed. The symbol, like the company, should be changed in response to changing markets and changing times.

chapter 5

Architecture and Store Plans

The aim of a successful store design, in order of importance, is to attract, identify, and merchandise. Any one of these areas cannot work without the others. If the unit attracts without identifying, the firm loses the repeat business. If it identifies without merchandising, it loses potential sales. One cannot merchandise without first getting attention, and then identifying the wares. Each works with the other, or one can neutralize the effect of the other two. The physical plant is therefore the principle means of communication. Often, the architecture and signs are the first selling points seen by the consumer. If they are not an inviting sight, no amount of in-store merchandising will lure the potential customer.

No matter what image the company seeks to establish, good design should not be sacrificed. Making the store attractive should not be thought of as a concession to environmentalists, but rather as the powerful merchandising tool it can be. An attractive, well-kept store tells the customer that the owners care about their customers and that they think enough of them to try to make them comfortable, honored guests.

ADVANTAGES OF GOOD STORE DESIGN

In April 1973, the first Federal Design Assembly met in Washington, D.C. The program, entitled "The Design Necessity," sought to prove that (1) effective design of public services is in itself a public service; (2) design is not a luxury or cosmetic addition; and (3) good design can save money and time and enhance the effectiveness of federal programs. The scope of this conference was focused on federal programs, but the points the initiators made apply to all forms of business. They made the following statements about design:

1. There are sound, proven criteria for judging design effectiveness.
2. Design can save money.
3. Design can save time.
4. Design enhances communications.
5. Design simplifies use, simplifies manufacture, simplifies maintenance.

As used in this book and as defined by the Design Assembly, the word *design* means a plan that is formed with an objective purpose in mind, for a specific reason. Whenever this planning is done, time and money are not wasted as they are when no plans are made, when individual problems are resolved in a piecemeal fashion, or when these individually resolved problems cause overlapping work or cancel each other out.

A good design plan would aim for making the exterior signs enhance the environment, relate to advertisements, relate to the interiors or help the interiors so that each would build on the other to strengthen the image. This facilitates customer recall and enhances communications.

Thinking and planning allows the management to foresee long-range problems and solutions. Good design simplifies whenever possible. If making fixtures alike throughout the store will allow mass production, which lowers costs and simplifies manufacture, the good designer and planner will do so. Simple, easy to care for, long lasting materials would be a part of a good design scheme, also, as they would lower maintenance costs and simplify maintenance.

Once the benefits of good design and an overall design plan are understood, the criteria for judging design effectiveness are obvious: if the

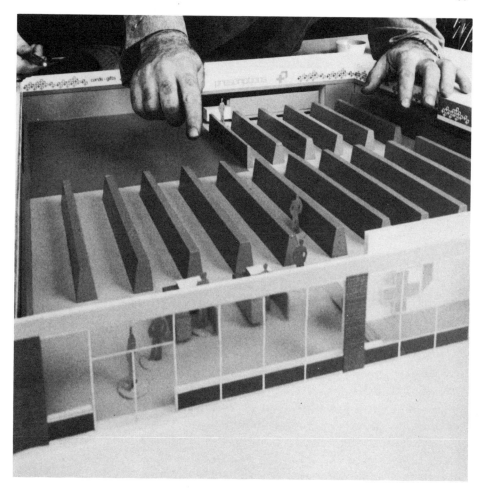

Figure 5-1 Developing a prototype model provides the designer and management the opportunity to see how well the design works. Refinements can easily and inexpensively be made at this stage. When Purity Supreme, a New England supermarket chain, entered the drug, health, and beauty aids field, they wanted to fulfill the following requirements: (1) to be able to realize the design concept within ten months; (2) to have simple design elements so that the chain could build each new store quickly at minimum expense with minimum variation; and (3) to project a store image of competitive prices and top quality. The prototype allowed them to realize all three objectives. Designer: Selame Design Associates.

design saves time, saves money, enhances communications, and simplifies manufacture and maintenance, then the design is effective. If the profit and loss statement does not change after the work is complete or even while the new materials are being ordered for new units, then the exercise in change has been a waste of time and money.

Of course, the store becomes the packaged product, and as such it is either saleable or not. Just as careful planning goes into package design to attract, identify, and merchandise, so it should go into store design. The ultimate reason for good store design is that it helps sell the product.

EXTERIOR DESIGN

As more and more commercial operations take to our major highways, it has become increasingly important for the structure to convey an identification quickly and legibly. When a store is being built from scratch, the architect and corporate design consultant can collaborate in developing a tasteful unit that meets zoning and building codes, is eye-catching, and that portrays the desired image to the passer-by.

However, with codes getting stricter and the cost of materials and labor spiralling upward, many operations are taking over existing structures whenever possible. The challenge for them is to make changes to attain the company's identity without completely rebuilding. For chain operations, there are added decisions: should the firm develop a prototype or work with existing buildings that will suit their space requirements? Should these existing buildings be given complete facelifts, or will adding just a few design elements carry through the identity? Should they change the prototype to suit each area of the country? Will these changes be a matter of efficiency, or part of the overall customer relations and identity program? (It should be both.) The Shell Oil Company adapts the architectural style of its stations to fit the local area. There are ranch-style stations, nine modern versions, Colonial versions, and hacienda versions. The unifying factor is the Shell symbol.

Making the shape of the exterior building a part of the identity limits the possibilities for taking over old stores. However, this is rarely a factor. It is difficult to devise a hard-and-fast prototype for other reasons, though. The land available, even for new units, is usually limited. The store might have to be modified to leave enough land in the proper configuration for parking, entrances, and traffic flow. If the chain store wants to open new units in a shopping center, the building is again limited to size and appearance by the design allowances set up by the center developer.

For these reasons, it is better to concentrate on square footage, colors, materials, and ambience for any prototype plans, or for any store exterior. A facade can be added to any building to accomodate the identity if the design specifications are limited to materials. The biggest danger here is that materials often become "faddish." For example, one company might erect an attractive store or remodel an existing unit using a certain type of stone. The effect is unique at the time, so other stores in the area jump on the bandwagon and remodel using the same material. No one has a corner on a building prototype or material. However, if the signage is distinctive (see Chapter 6) and the windows clearly display the merchandise or interior, no one will be able to achieve the same look. For these reasons, within the restrictions of local laws, any exterior design should make the most of the company's biggest distinction—the symbol. (See Figure 5-2.)

PROJECTING PRICE IMAGE

When discount stores began opening in old Quonset huts or factories, it was easy for any passer-by to tell they were discount stores. However, many discounters are no longer convinced that a plain exterior will portray a low-price image *and* attract customers. Consumers like to shop in attractive stores, no matter what they are paying for the merchandise. It is possible and desirable to upgrade the architecture and interior and still portray low prices. A discounter would not want to face his store with marble, but a shabby exterior often connotes poor quality to the modern shopper. Remember, the image is as important as the merchandise.

Good, simple design will connote good quality at low prices, just as lush design should connote high quality at medium or high prices. All architecture should be designed well; the details and the materials used are the factors that should differ for varying price images. (See Figure 5-3.) Besides the design for the basic structure, there are other factors to consider in the exterior plans:

1. Landscaping—This is an area often overlooked entirely or left to the last minute. Many zoning codes now require the developers to add greenery, but it still is often an afterthought instead of an integral part of the exterior design. Well-kept grounds, foliage, and plantings can establish an image of permanence and success even before the shopper enters the store. A good landscape architect can often soften the look of a concrete fortress; in fact, if an un-

Figure 5-2A Shaw's old exterior lacked distinction from other similar stores.

Figure 5-2B Shaw's new exterior makes the most of the company's distinction: its symbol. The image is reinforced by use of the symbol inside the store. Designer: Selame Design Associates.

Figure 5-3 Tagway uses bold yet simple design to portray its price image and reach the desired market. Utilizing the familiarity of orange-tag sales, an orange tag carrying the newly coined name "Tagway" speaks honestly for the store's products, which are fashionable yet economical shoes for the whole family. Carrying through this theme on the interior store design, take-out packages, labels, ads, and other promotional material has provided management with basic marketing tools. Designer: Selame Design Associates.

attractive building is taken over in lieu of building a new store, the landscaping can often change the whole look to conform to your image. The landscaping can be simple for stores wishing to portray low-price image; grass, some low hedges at the perimeter of the grass, and some trees within the green area are sufficient to make the area look alive without making it look elaborately designed. The landscaping should be more elaborate for stores wishing to portray higher-price images. Sculpture and other embellishments can also help portray high-price images. However, all greenery and other additions must be chosen for the best effect with the least maintenance. The plants chosen must be suited to the climate; a dead tree or brown shrubs will only make the store look dead. Sculpture, pebbles, and so on should be firmly fixed and be of sturdy material in order to prevent damage from traffic flow, weather conditions, and possible vandalism.

2. Parking lot—This should be treated as a part of the store. It should be well illuminated for security and customer convenience no matter what the image of the store. The area markers should be simple and easy to remember, and designed to enhance the image and reflect the identity. There are several systems that can be used to code parking areas, such as numbers, letters, or symbols. The easiest to remember devices are color-coded symbols. These symbols can be either the corporate symbol made of materials to reflect the image, or related symbols that enhance the image of the store (see Figure 5-4).

3. Display windows—With the price of dressing and maintaining these windows ever higher, many discounters do not use them. Others are finding alternatives, such as large windows that expose the store's interior and therefore do not need dressing. These are very effective at night, when the store becomes the show, in color and motion. These would also reflect any price image, as they expose the store's interior design to the passer-by.

4. Public accomodations—This includes exterior seating and other public conveniences such as phone booths. A higher-

Figure 5-4   Finding your way back to the car is easy in Oshawa's Montreal hypermarché. The parking lot area markers are easy to spot and leave the customer nothing to remember but an animal symbol.

price store, which usually operates at a lower-key pace, would reflect this by providing benches or other areas where the customers could relax while shopping or waiting for public transportation.

Whatever the exterior, it should be functional and durable. The design does not have to (and probably should not) stay the same for the life of the company, but the material should not start falling apart or showing wear before a change is desired. No matter how beautiful the basic design, if the material or any part of the building starts looking shabby, it will depress rather than entice the customer.

For example, in areas of heavy rain or extreme heat, wood exteriors will show wear very quickly. Shingles or panels will fade and warp easily in these climates, unless properly treated for protection. In metropolitan areas with a large amount of air pollution, porous light exteriors tend to look grimy quickly. No matter what the climate, some materials show wear faster than others, and the designer and architect should consider this factor in choosing materials.

INTERIOR DESIGN

If the store is not attracting customers, new paint on the walls will not solve the problem. The store is either not capturing the customer's imagination or it is confusing the shopper. When remodeling to solve one or both of these problems, some things might be salvaged or the interior can be ripped out completely and begun from scratch. In many cases, it is less expensive to gut a store and start all over. In some cases (for example, when the interior is attractive, but confusing), adding a few design elements might be the solution.

Whichever method is chosen, why re-invent the wheel? If time saving and a limited budget are called for, pick existing fixtures and standard materials. The designer might have to search through twenty catalogs to find what he is looking for, but he will eventually find fixtures to suit his design. There are four qualities available to all if the effort is put forth:

1. Function (this is evident—the function is always available)
2. Price (mass production will lower the price)
3. Durability (fragile fixtures will need repair, which wastes time and money)

4.   Availability (if the fixtures are not made to order, they will be available faster and for longer periods of time, in most cases)

Rather than spending large amounts of money, pick existing fixtures and put the money into decor details that project the visual identity. Non-custom fixtures will not be innovative in themselves, but they can be innovative in their application. In other words, the fixtures that hold the merchandise are less important than the way in which they hold the merchandise, and how much merchandise they hold. The type of fixtures can connote the type of store if they are chosen conventionally: for example, tables usually identify department or variety stores; gondolas are found in grocery and discount stores; and so on. There is no rule that this has to be the case; a departure from the norm might be the innovation that the customer is looking for. However, a departure should not be made for its own sake. The fixture has to be functional. It is also important to remember that except for table bases or show cases, little fixture shows when the merchandise is added. The colors and textures are therefore more important than the fixture itself.

A well thought out design considers both availability and price of materials as well as their aesthetic value. If a prototype design is developed for a chain operation, then thought should be given to developing "plug-in" units. (See Figures 5-5 and 5-6.) The more of the store decor that can be mass-produced at one time, the less per unit it will cost, and the less time it will take to remodel or open up new units.

Ceilings

The basic elements of any interior—ceilings, floors, and walls—are often not given the attention they deserve and are often not used to the fullest potential. A pretty ceiling will not sell much more merchandise, but a drab ceiling will take away from the total look of the store. The "T-bar" grid is the most often used ceiling pattern in most large stores today. It is inexpensive because it is standard, but it is also effective. However, there are many variations in textures and acoustical qualities available to fit this pattern. If the store is large and plain, the ceiling can be used to break up this feeling or to achieve a boutique look. The introduction of coves, cove lighting, or a change in planes can add interest. The strength of the ceiling can be the lighting, another important factor in the ambience of the store. The company might want a brightly lit interior, which is often the case in

Figure 5-5 You & You uses molded acrylic signs designed to strongly identify the retailer both outside and inside the store. These plug-ins allow the company to order bulk quantities in advance and plug in the wall decor, no matter how long or short the store footage is. Designer: Selame Design Associates.

discount stores, or it might want a subdued, rosy lighting effect, which might be the case for a store in the top price range.

The ceiling can also be used to advantage when the floor space is limited. It can be used for hanging displays, for directional signing, for department-name signs, and so on. For example, Bradlees uses ceiling-hung graphics to identify their 56 departments. They had 4-foot by 6-foot panels silk screened with bold lettering and splashes of color to identify the departments and the major seasons (winter and summer). The panels are light weight and can be easily turned for the seasonal changes. They have

Figure 5-6A The universal symbol for health, the cross, was incorporated with the letter "P" to form Pharmacity's symbol. A cluster of these symbols is used in the overall signage system, which identifies the company, identifies the departments within the store through color coding, and is the major interior design element. The signage can be mass produced and plugged in to new units. Designer: Selame Design Associates.

Figure 5-6B On all peripheral walls, color-coded symbols on a white background tell the customer at a glance where to find the gift area (blue and green), prescriptions (blue and red), tobacco (brown and burnt orange), beauty center (white "p's" on a magenta background). In a one-step process using colorful preformed panels, identifying decor and departmental signage are available to this chain.

the added flexibility that allows store managers to do a little creative work of their own. They can be hung back to back, adjacent to each other, at right angles, or staggered in and out. They are prominent enough so that the customers can easily locate the merchandise they are looking for, and they are attractive. They give the interior the distinctive decor the company wanted, and they are modern and interesting. (See Figures 5-7A through 5-7C.)

Floors

The floors can be covered in carpeting, tile, terrazzo, asphalt tile; it will depend on how much money is budgeted for installation and for maintenance. Carpeting often looks clean even after a day of heavy traffic, and many feel it is easier and less expensive to maintain than are other materials. However, this fact is often not obvious to consumers, who might feel that some of their shopping dollar is going into a lush carpet. So, a discounter might want to install tile or linoleum instead. There are so many floor coverings to choose from that anyone can find a material at the right price that will suit the identity program. The material should be chosen for color and the added effect to the total store package.

If the company is working with boutiques, then the different floor areas can be covered in different materials to help separate the departments and give them each their own identity. For example, if the store carries two lines of clothing, one low price and the other more expensive, the floors of these areas can be covered to help accentuate the difference: the low-price clothing area can be covered in tile, and the more-expensive area can be carpeted. Tiles of different colors can also be used for in-store directionals. This is especially effective when the different department signs are color coded. But remember that once the floors are color coded, department flexibility (such as moves when one department needs more space) is severely limited.

Walls

To many designers, the walls are their canvas. Walls are also valued highly for decor possibilities by the retailers who use them for their strongest merchandise projection. Up to about 7 feet from the floor, the walls are usually hidden by the merchandise displays, but above that, there are almost no restrictions. Department signage can be used; displays of merchandise to identify the departments can be hung on the walls; colors can be used to set moods for different departments. There are limitless

Figure 5-7A Bradlees makes the most of its ceiling space by hanging identifying panels over each department. The signs are functional, attractive, and easy to move around. Designer: Selame Design Associates.

Figure 5-7B

74

Figure 5-7C

Figure 5-8A Shaw's color codes its interior walls for departmental differentiation and uses its symbol and signature typeface for the departmental signage. This helps enhance the image as it reinforces the identity, and affords the savings of mass production. Designer: Selame Design Associates.

Figure 5-8B Shaw's dairy department exemplifies how well the walls are used without being cluttered or monotonous.

possibilities for this area, but the designer should keep his work here in line with the projected personality. The space should be used, but not cluttered, as that would again tend to confuse the customers. Also, any decor details added to walls should probably be flexible enough to change with the seasons or with department moves within the store. Structurally, the walls connect the ceiling and floor; they should connect them in design, also, to unify and complete the in-store identity.

For example, the Mister Donut Shops cover their walls with vinyl depicting giant-sized doughnuts in their color scheme of deep chocolate and cinnamon (see Figure 5-9). This is a graphically simple but easily understood statement of product. It can be seen through their glass-front exterior, helping even the passer-by on the highway to know what the shop is there for. If any statement, interior or exterior, can be made without words, make that statement graphically. It makes it pleasant yet easy for the customer of any background or age to understand and enjoy.

Changing Interiors

With the new modular walls and fixtures, an interior of any store could conceivably be changed completely in twenty-four hours. It might make a nice change for the retailers and their employees, but is it a good change for the customers? If the interior of the store has been carefully planned to state the company's identity and the products they sell, and the plan has been accepted and learned by the customer, then this type of radical change might be bad for the business. It can be very confusing to the customer who knows where to find the desired merchandise. If the customer was happy with things in a certain place, then the change might discourage him from coming back.

If, on the other hand, the store needs a new identity, this modular change might be the way to go to avoid long periods of construction that interfere with the normal flow of business. After the major structural changes have been made, then the company can take its time adding the decor details that make the store's distinctive personality.

Designing for Security

A good corporate design program will also help the store in a less obvious area—pilferage. As the assessment of the current interior or the plans for the new one are made, the designer and architect should check into building in elements to discourage thefts by employees and customers.

Figure 5-9 The Mister Donut shop interiors explain the function of the stores without words and are visible even to the passer-by. Designer: Selame Design Associates.

For example, the planners can design the location of registers, television surveillance cameras, and stock areas for easy observation, which discourages would-be thieves. A sound design will also eliminate non-observable areas and provide enough space in stockrooms so that all merchandise can be put away properly. Anything out of place would be easily observable, and anything easily observable is usually a detriment to pilferage. Organized displays, boldly visible display areas, and even carefully planned packaging can all discourage thefts. So, these design elements would not only be attractive and integral to the interior identity, but they could also help the shrinkage plaguing all phases of business today.

SHOPPING CENTERS: WHOSE IDENTITY, DEVELOPER'S OR RETAILERS'?

The most essential ingredient to the success of the shopping center is the excitement distilled by an environment conducive to social intercourse and visual variety. For years, there was such a large demand for retail centers from the new mobile population that almost any shopping strip or center, no matter how badly designed, became a goldmine. When a few more progressive developers began to create more inviting environments, their message spread with such speed that everyone to some extent or another followed suit. And there has been little innovation since the 1950s. The latest in centers now are still copies of the older centers, but on a larger and ever-growing scale. How large is too large will be an important question soon.

The once loosely amalgamated shopping center is now comprised of retailers who join together in order to develop property that is outside the hearts of cities and towns, and they are now becoming the cities and towns of America. The developers whose only interest at one time was to provide housing for retailers are now involved with providing a social, economic, and political environment for thousands of people. Regional malls are now built as total entities, a slice of our cities. Some centers can now fulfill an individual's entire needs, practically from cradle to grave. In some of these self-contained units are apartments, medical clinics, hotels, religious centers, libraries, nurseries, schools, and retail stores of every description, all with temperature and humidity control.

In order to compete and differentiate their developments from others, developers are attempting to provide added attractions to their

Figure 5-10 Crown Center, Kansas City's $200 million city within a city, will be a total entity when complete in 1983. It includes office buildings, retail complexes, apartments, a hotel, and tree-lined streets. Designer: Hallmark Cards, Inc., and Edward Larrabee Barnes, FAIA.

centers, such as interiors that contain Greek amphitheaters, ice skating rinks, aviaries, and aquariums. Unfortunately, these methods, which should be added touches, are often thought of by the developers to be the main identification. However, as more of these amphitheaters, circuses, and floor shows appear, they will serve only to confuse the customers. Unless the architecture, interior, promotion, and graphics all play the same theme, nothing, except perhaps chaos, will be communicated. This will help the customers form a negative image without any identity, and therefore hurt the center and the retailers in the center.

The developer of the center naturally wants his property to be seen, recognized, and remembered. In order to achieve this, a commitment to a visual shopping center identity program has to be made. The best time to do this is before ground is broken. An expression of identity through a name and graphic theme can be useful to the developer at the very outset in order to help him merchandise to prospective tenants, and the more successful the merchandiser, the more successful will be the mix of tenants. First, of course, the developer has to decide, perhaps with marketing research and economic analysis consultants, what the most profitable shopping center mix should be in a given area. This in turn should determine the desired image of the center as a total unit. Then the architectural qualifications, the name, and the graphic identification of the center can be conceptualized. The identity program is then developed in the same manner as it would be for a retailer.

The name of the development should be one of the most important considerations of the developer, yet it is one that is usually overlooked. Choosing a name that pinpoints the center's location has been the old standby. This has often led to the center being identified as a place to shop the anchor stores, rather than by the name of the center. A symbol for the shopping center should be created and used on all visual material, again, as it would be used by any company. It should be considered as important as any corporation's symbol. It is important to note that the best designed symbols will not fulfill their intended goals if they are not consistently used on all visible aspects of the program.

However, promoting the center without also promoting its tenants can be a mistake. A major retailing research study found that shopping malls do have identity problems. If the individuality of each retailer is not strongly emphasized in signage, interiors, and other architectural and graphic media, the consumers can feel that they are in one large department store. Too often, a sale is lost because the customer "loses his way." And, if the tenants lose enough sales because they cannot advertise their

Figure 5-11A The White Plains Mall is symbolized by an abstract tree form. The exterior free-standing sculpture signage combines a row of trees with the word "Mall." A lollipop-shaped tree has become the background silhouette for the individual shop symbols used to designate the different stores; a further simplification of the lollipop shape can be seen within the sculpture. Designer: Wyman & Cannan Co. of New York.

Figure 5-11B The lollipop symbols, when applied to shopping bags and the mall directory as well, combine into a large tree on a mural in the central court of the mall. Chrome metallic tree-shaped symbols with white silk-screened pictorial images in the center make up the 44-foot high tree emblazoned on the brightly painted yellow mall.

Figure 5-12 The shopping mall symbol and name are as important as those of any company. A new shopping center in Oahu, Hawaii, is located outside of Pearl City. The name chosen was Pearlridge Mall, and the symbol was formed by a spiral of black pearls of increasing size, which also form an abstract "P." The combination of the name, symbol, and the carefully designed signage system work together to make both the symbol and the name of the mall memorable. Design Director: Robert P. Gersin Associates Inc. Pictures reproduced by permission of the design director.

presence in the center by expressing their own identity, the center will lose the tenants when their leases are up or when they go out of business.

The problem is complex. If the center is totally unified visually, it can be monotonous or confusing, and the tenants will lose their identities if they have not already forfeited these to comply with the center's visual specifications. On the other hand, if the center allows tenants a completely free hand in the store's design, it runs the risk of looking like a carnival. Too much visual stimulation can be as confusing and annoying to the customer as too little.

There are those developers who leave everything up to the retailer's tastes and needs, and there are developers who prohibit all exterior signs except for the major department stores and for the mall itself. Some signage codes allow store identification as long as they conform in

Figure 5-13 The Pearlridge symbol became an intricate part of the mall's identity system from the beginning. In order to make the center more attractive during the construction of various store fronts, a barricade system was designed and the symbol displayed on the barricade. The left side of the picture above shows completed stores, and the right shows the barricade and symbol. Design Director: Robert P. Gersin Associates Inc. Pictures reproduced by permission of the design director.

overall color scheme, dimensions, and materials. This allows the tenants to identify themselves but eliminates the risk of a carnival atmosphere and helps unify the center's visual identity.

Some design criteria must be established, if the developer does not want a shopping center that soon looks like a hodgepodge. However, it

Figure 5-14 In Salem, New Hampshire, a new mall was named after the area's best-known leisure area, the Rockingham Park race track; its location was therefore pinpointed by its name. The developers dropped the "Park" in order to not confuse the mall with the track. Using the archway theme, the designers depicted the initials "R" and "M" by juxtaposing three arches. For exterior signage, a stark white symbol lies on a black flocked background for strong visibility. Interior and exterior wall graphics carry the theme into various design patterns. Designer: Selame Design Associates.

Figure 5-15   An exterior concrete wall in the Rockingham Mall offered the possibility of identifying the mall and/or Bradlees. With the cooperation of Bradlees, both were identified, with the mall's name in larger letters. The mall's symbol is repeated on the remainder of the wall. By making this choice, the retailer and the mall are both made known, avoiding the feeling of "one big department store."

is important that the individual tenants retain separate and distinct personalities. It is an advantage that all will share. Visual variety helps create the excitement and social intercourse so necessary to the life of the center. The prospective tenants should investigate what restrictions have been established. If they are too rigid, the retailers should either object or not rent the space. If enough companies do this, the center developer might soften the restrictions, to everyone's advantage. The retailers should also object to design codes that are too loosely formed, for the same reasons—it will hurt business.

The shopping center has to balance the need for order against the need for flexibility. It has to balance the need of the center's overall objectives against the needs and desires of individual retailers. If this balance is successfully made, the various parts of the center are capable of building a successful unit.

Figure 5-16 Utilizing Rockingham Mall's symbol as interior wall decor does not interfere with the retailers' identities, yet it unifies the identity of the mall itself.

Figure 5-17 Because its design system was so carefully planned, the White Plains Mall can even identify mall and retailer successfully in newspaper advertisements. Each retailer displays his own name and symbol, but the ad is bordered by the mall's tree symbol. Even the map at the top left uses a small symbol to pinpoint the location.

chapter 6

Exterior Signage

Peter Blake, in the preface to his book, *God's Own Junkyard: The Planned Deterioration of America's Landscape*, states that he is deliberately attacking "all those who have already befouled a large portion of this country for private gain...People whose eyes have lost the art of seeing... and...all of us who no longer care, or no longer care enough."[1]

"Freedom to communicate is basic to our society. Freedom of speech, freedom to be heard, also implies freedom to be seen." (Outdoor Advertising, Inc.)

These two quotes characterize the two bitterly opposed sides of the current signage debate. Which side is winning? Which opinion represents the future? Which opinion reflects a passing era? A quick look at this debate over the years follows:

In 1905, a New Jersey court said, "Aesthetic considerations are a matter of luxury and indulgence rather than of necessity."

In 1937, the Court of Appeals of New York held invalid an ordinance of the city of Troy that forbade all billboards except those on the same premises on which the business advertised was located.

[1] (New York: Holt, Rinehart, and Winston, 1964), p.7.

In 1954, the U.S. Supreme Court said, "It is within the power of the legislature to determine that the community should be beautiful."

In 1968, the operator of a service station and restaurant on the west side of a highway in Wallkill, New York, began to put up two signs on land he owned on the east side of the highway and was stopped by the local building inspector. He challenged the constitutionality of the local ordinance that allowed the inspector to stop him. He based his case largely on the 1937 case concerning Troy, New York. After a trial and two appeals, the courts still ruled against him. The Court of Appeals overruled its 1937 decision, saying that circumstances, surrounding conditions, changed social attitudes, and newly acquired knowledge do not alter the Constitution, but they do alter the view of what is reasonable. The court also felt that advertising signs and billboards, if misplaced, often are a conglomerate of ugliness, distraction, and deterioration; so, they are just as much subject to reasonable controls, including prohibition, as enterprises that emit offensive noises, odors, or debris.

The trend has clearly been toward more signage control, and in some localities these controls are very detailed. And, they are enforced. If these changes in the law are not a convincing argument against aesthetically offensive signs, think of this: laws are not created or changed until a great need arises. This need can only be determined by the number of people in the community calling for the change or the number of people affected by the current condition. That growing public concern for all aspects of environmental and business controls is a fact can be seen by looking at the growth of groups lobbying for these changes.

A company can win a signage fight in court and lose in the store. No matter what the local laws are, no business can risk a bad public image. If the population is concerned about the appearance of their area, the business should seek their approval by redesigning garish or poorly placed signage. If a customer first encounters a company's name on a remote sign and the sign is offensive, that customer might never enter that store. Good signage is a matter of good advertising and good public relations, just as is the whole identity program.

CORPORATE IDENTITY PROGRAMS HELP CLEAN UP SIGNS

A good sign is functional, shows good design, establishes the identity of the displayer, is visible, and abides by all the ordinances. A good graphic designer can satisfy the company and the inspector when he creates the exterior signage as an integral part of the identity program.

Figure 6-1A This Bradlees was one of the original discount department stores acquired by The Stop & Shop Companies. With no symbol and no memorable signature, extra verbiage with no distinction results on the signage.

With the use of the corporate symbol, he can reduce the verbiage on the sign, make it striking and distinctive without being garish, and even reduce the size of the sign without decreasing the readability. He can satisfy his sense of aesthetics and the company's call for readability. (See Figure 6-1.)

When first developing the program, one of the criteria for picking the symbol, as mentioned earlier in this book, is that it be as effective at a fraction of a inch as it is twenty feet high. If this is the case, then it is effective at any size: it is readable, it identifies the company, and it is eye catching. (See Figure 6-2.) If the local ordinances call for signs only two feet square, a good sign can be created that will catch the public eye if the symbol is a prominent part of that sign. Many ordinances demand that the on-site sign be an integral part of the store's architecture. (See Figure 6-3.) Many stores have done this for years by placing their signatures in raised letters right on the building itself. A symbol can be fashioned the same way for the same effect. There is nothing sticking up into the air, there are no flashing lights. At night, these letters or symbols can be tastefully well lit by the use of some flood lights on the ground. When working with a few design elements that tell most of the story, any zoning code, no matter how

Figure 6-1B After a corporate identity program, Bradlees' store fronts are attractive and distinctive. The Bradlees signage is a modified Folio typeface fabricated from stainless steel. The letters are set on a 20-foot by 100-foot backdrop of white porcelain enamel panels, false edged to simulate granite blocks without the weight burden of the real stone. Each letter is 8 to 10 inches deep, illuminated by white neon tubing and faced with aquamarine plastic. The large sign is supported on an all welded angle iron, channel iron, and H-beam structure. The black steel supports were designed to be an integral part of the whole sign. Below and running perpendicular to the larger sign are scaled-down signs to give the illusion of added support and dimension. These signs are double-faced porcelain enamel with pegged-out porcelain enamel letters. The "B" is red-orange, chrome yellow, and aquamarine. This sign serves as an identification when viewed approaching the entrance at a closer range. Designer: Selame Design Associates.

Figure 6-2A A Mister Donut shop before the corporate identity program. The signs are neither attractive nor easily legible to passers-by.

Figure 6-2B A Mister Donut in Pompano, Florida, after the corporate identity program. The signage is simpler, easier to read, and more attractive. The symbol, shown on the sign and in a repetitive pattern across the exterior, cuts down on sign verbiage and is eye catching. It is used on all Mister Donut visual material. Designer: Selame Design Associates.

Figure 6-3　If local ordinances demand that the exterior signage be an integral part of the architecture, there are many solutions. In the case of Alperts furniture warehouse, the building is the sign, and so this restriction did not affect a new location identity as much as it might have otherwise. A bold red-orange "A" on a white background with a directional arrow pointing to the front door is highly visible and attractive even from the highway. Designers: Selame Design Associates.

restrictive, can be met. If the company needs several pictures or many words to tell their story, they will have problems as the codes get more protective.

Sign manufacturers have made great progress in the technology of signage. New materials permit more durable signs that require less maintenance. But technology alone is not the answer; there are old signs that, with proper maintenance, would serve well for another twenty years. Any well constructed sign should last well over ten years. The difference between the eye catcher and the eyesore is one of design. No sign that is illegible or makes poor or garish use of color and typography is good just because it uses the most modern technology. No sign is considered a blight on the area because it is large, although a large, poorly designed sign is more of an eyesore than is a smaller version of the same sign. Good design does not necessarily mean sterility. Visual excitement is good for business and entertaining for the viewer. (See Figure 6-4.) There is nothing inherently wrong with neon or with bright colors or with a very large sign. In fact, neon might be the ideal medium in the future. It is long lasting and uses very little energy for its light source. Several young artists have recently begun creating neon sculpture that proves the medium can be beautiful, if well designed. The designer can choose the modern technology, but first he must choose the right design. His task is made much simpler by the well-designed corporate symbol. (See Figure 6-5.)

The most important functions of a sign are identification and communication, and the tool of communication is typography. Too often, these functions and their tool are lost in the effort to be "creative" or "dramatic." All good typography and design have one thing in common: easy readability. An easily readable, simple sign is much more dramatic than any other kind, and it serves its purposes of identification and communication. (See Figure 6-6.) If the symbol is used as the central design element of the sign, it can be recognized quickly, understood quickly, and it lessens the need for other elements on the sign. Simplicity can be beautiful and dramatic, with the careful use of colors. However, as the symbol, the colors to be used in its reproduction, and the other identifying elements of the company are established with the initial design, the sign just about designs itself. The same design elements appearing on the letterhead can be used for the on-site signs. The firm might or might not add extra information, such as address, store hours, and so on, on its remote signage.

Figure 6-4 Good looking signs are an asset to the environment and need not be small. The sign for Lawry's Restaurant in Los Angeles, California, can be seen from a great distance. Designer: Saul Bass and Associates.

Research

When the graphic designer is first called in and begins his research into the needs of the company for its new identity, he should

Figure 6-5   A well-designed symbol can conform to any zoning code and still make an attractive sign. In Carmel, California, restrictive codes do not allow the use of internally lit signs. Shell creatively resolved this problem by using native redwood and gold leaf lettering to form their symbol and sign. Picture courtesy of the Shell Oil Company.

Figure 6-6A When stricter architectural and signage codes become law in an area, many companies fear that removal of large signs that were put up prior to the laws will have to be replaced by small, non-identifiable, invisible signs to conform to the codes. The Charlestown Savings Bank's old signage was large without being particularly easy to read.

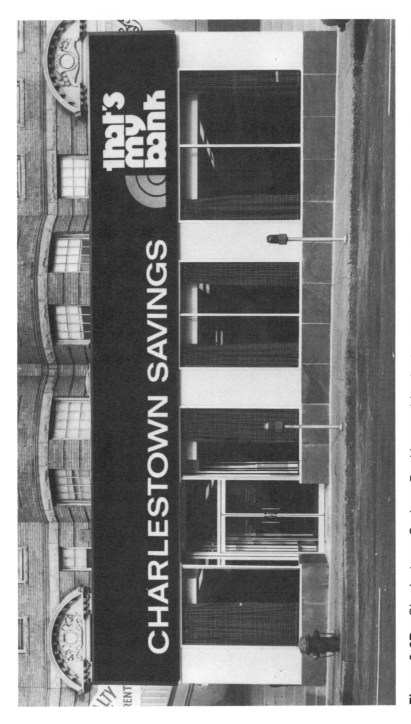

Figure 6-6B Charlestown Savings Bank's new identity incorporates a bold magenta mark of three concentric "C's" and "Charlestown Savings, that's my bank" in white type on a black background. Although the new sign is bolder and more visible than the old one, the zoning board welcomes it because its good design—fewer, cleaner lines—enhances the community. Designer: Selame Design Associates.

Figure 6-7 In Peachtree Center, Atlanta, Georgia, Franklin Simon was confronted with an interesting problem that the designers innovatively resolved. To announce the second-floor store from the street, an outside elevator carries the store name and its symbol, a butterfly. The Franklin Simon logo appears over the elevator entrance and is repeated in a spiral around the plexiglass column, serving the dual purpose of exterior and interior identification. Symbol Design: Seymour Chwast and Milton Glaser. Store and Graphic Design: George Nelson & Company.

research every aspect of the program, including what laws are in effect that restrict or in any other way affect the signage. A competent designer will know these codes or have easy access to them, and he should be charged with the responsibility of making sure the signs will abide by the ordinances. Because there are so many variations in sign code ordinances, the established design must be flexible and adaptable to any condition that might arise. It is the designer's job to see to it that the sign looks attractive horizontally or vertically, large or small. Established chain operations have put major effort behind marketing the differences between their company and others. If their exterior identity is outlawed, a good percentage of the time and money put into strong corporate identity is wasted. It is extremely important to research and plan all facets of the program at the same time.

Figure 6-8 The large symbol seen from the street is silk screened on both the glass cab of the elevator and the smoky plexiglass enclosure, which creates a fluttering action when the elevator moves. This signage solution is both attractive and unique. Designer: George Nelson & Company.

And it is very important to test the look and the legality of the symbol for all parts of the program.

Technology

There are many media that can be used to make signs: plastics, metal, neon or other gas-filled tubing, decals, stencils, and so on. Each material can be worked into a sign by many processes. For example, plastics can be vacuum formed, molded, die cut, engraved, sandblasted

Figure 6-9 The inside elevator entrance on the second floor is dominated by the Franklin Simon butterfly on a deep mauve wall. Composed of vertical fins edged in chrome, each face of the battens is painted a different color: mauve, green, or blue. As shoppers pass the symbol in either direction, the color changes produce the same fluttering motion created by the elevator. The store logo appears on both sides of the symbol. A low, purple vinyl-upholstered bench makes elevator-waiting comfortable. Designer: George Nelson & Company.

through a stencil, cut, or silk screened. With all the forms to choose from, the designer can meet any sign code and still express the identity of the company and his aesthetic values. For example, if the local ordinances prohibit exterior signs that extend above the building or that are not an integral part of the building, there are many options. Besides the raised letters or symbols placed on the building, a sign can be stenciled, painted, or otherwise placed inside a large display window and lit with interior or exterior lighting. (See Figures 6-7, 6-8, and 6-9.) It can be built into the exterior wall by several means and lit with an interior light source. The possibilities go on and on.

However, many of these forms of sign making are in danger of dying out with the sign craftsmen, who are becoming an endangered species. If trained graphic designers could learn some of the techniques of sign making, they could couple this knowledge with their design talent to create exciting, varied signs that would satisfy the environmentalists, the businessmen, and the designers alike. This cannot happen, of course, unless the designers take the initiative and seek the knowledge or unless businessmen who use the designers' services start asking to see the signage possibilities in all media.

> The design of commercial signs in America is a kind of surviving folk art. There are no prominent sign designers as there are, for example, prominent architects; there are no schools to educate sign designers; and very little has been published in the way of criticism or instruction in the art of sign design. Most of the expertise that exists is in effect a set of trade secrets of sign manufacturers. And yet, signs are almost as important in the cityscape as architecture; at night signs become the visible city.[2]

There is no reason for the technology to remain a trade secret; designers, their corporate customers, and the sign makers would all benefit financially from a renewed cooperation in the field of sign design and craftsmanship. The cities and mall areas would all benefit aesthetically.

SHOPPING CENTER DIRECTIONALS AND STORE SIGNS

Just as a store's signage is regarded and designed as an integral part of the overall architectural plans, the signage in shopping centers

---

[2] Alvin Eisenman, *Design Quarterly 92* (Minneapolis, Minn.: Walker Art Center, 1974), p. 2. This issue of the magazine was devoted to the research work into sign design done by the graphic design class at the Philadelphia College of Art, and would be of great interest to all graphic designers.

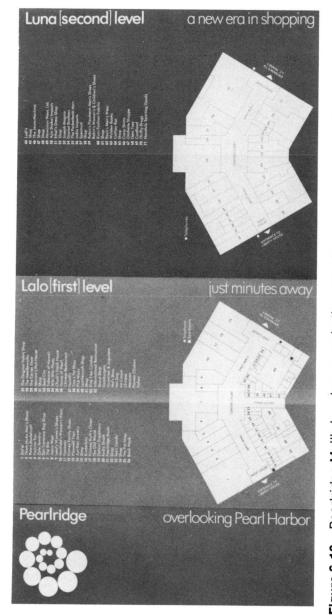

Figure 6-10 Pearlridge Mall's brochures are both promotional and informative. Simple and easy to read, they serve as mall directional signage. Design Director: Robert P. Gersin Associates Inc. Pictures reproduced by permission of the design director.

Figure 6-11 Closed, the Pearlridge brochure clearly indicates the name, place, and symbol of the mall and shows that the mall has two levels. Pictures reproduced by permission of the design director.

should be developed along with the architecture. Directional signs in the center should lead the customer into the mall, easily tell him where each store is located, and then lead him back to his car with the fewest possible steps. In many cases today, directional signage in centers is confusing or there is not enough of it.

Signage in centers does not have to be dull or uniform. (See Figure 6-14.) With color coding and prominent center identification, the signs can become interesting decorative elements. (See Figure 6-15.) The names of the stores in the center do not even have to be shown in the same type—each can use its own signature or symbol without being confusing if the signs are well designed. (See Figures 6-16 through 6-23.) The retailers in the center should be interested in whether there is sufficient directional signage and how clear it is because it will affect their businesses. They should also be interested in what the signs say, not just how they say it. Not all the directionals need to carry extensive information, but there should be easily accessible directories that give information about the stores as well as directions to them.

SUMMARY

In just a few years, if the establishment is not a visual asset to the environment, there will be very few welcome mats put out by the town fathers or by customers in other communities. An ugly sign or a court fight

Figure 6-12 In repetition, a symbol can serve as a directional sign. The College Town symbol, shown here in the New York City showroom, especially lends itself to this purpose. Designer: Selame Design Associates.

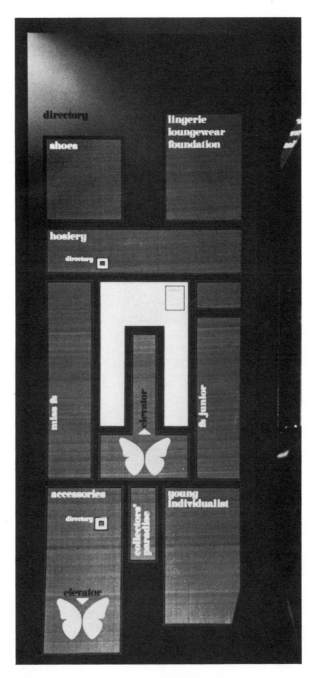

Figure 6-13 The simpler the store or mall directionals, the easier they are to understand. Pictorial or graphic directories are easy for anyone to read. The Franklin Simon directory in Peachtree Center is a floor plan of the store that makes use of the symbol and color scheme. Silk screened on a transluscent plexiglass column, the interior lighting makes the floor plan glow. Designer: George Nelson & Company.

Figure 6-14 Signage in malls does not have to be dull or uniform. Within designated limits, retailers at Paramus Park in New Jersey can create visual variety while maintaining a semblance of order and aesthetics. Design criteria established by The Rouse Company, developer/owner of Paramus Park.

Figure 6-15 Signs can become interesting decorative elements even when mall signage restrictions are great. When Bond's architectural firm found out that mall exterior signage restrictions would not fulfill the store's needs, they adapted a unique solution. As no restriction was placed on interior signage, Bond's identity was placed just inside the entrance in a highly visible way. Designer: Christopher & Gilbert Associates.

Figure 6-16 Pearlridge Mall's designers set up signage restrictions, but left the retailers several options for their exteriors. The designers wanted to create visual excitement while still allowing the center to have a distinct order in the way tenants designed their stores. Therefore, a special type of signage code was set up to regulate the way in which the tenants designed their stores and signs and to encourage them to integrate the signs and the storefronts. This enabled the tenants to put the signage wherever they chose: on the walls, the floor, or the ceiling. A grid or format was established, limiting the locations of typography, so that all mall typography would line up even though it was used in different styles, colors, scales, or areas. Here and in the next seven photographs, these options are seen to be great enough to allow expression of individual identity without creating a carnival atmosphere. Repetitive headband signage creates a design and lets the shoppers know the retailers name. Design Director: Robert P. Gersin Associates Inc. Pictures reproduced by permission of the design director.

Figure 6-17 This storefront eliminates headband signage by using interior-lit vertical signage. Design Director: Robert P. Gersin Associates Inc. Pictures reproduced by permission of the design director.

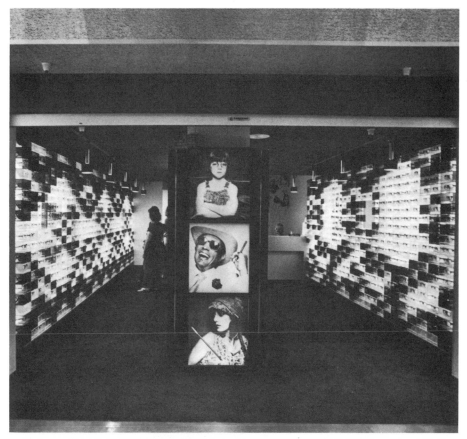

Figure 6-18 This retailer chose rear-illuminated transparencies as signage and identity, showing that the shoes he sells are for men, women, and children. Design Director: Robert P. Gersin Associates, Inc. Pictures reproduced by permission of the design director.

can ruin an otherwise good image. The signage must identify and attract—not identify and repel. With the use of the symbol, the signage can identify and create a positive image in the consumers' minds that will support and in turn be supported by the rest of the identity program.

In essence, a sign, whether remote or on-site, says, "Here we are." If the passers-by react to that statement with "So what," or, "Yes, but we wish you weren't," the signs are not serving their purpose. Signage should create a positive image that makes the customer want to enter the store, or that interests and informs him enough to come back when he does want to shop that type of store. If a sign is not memorable, making it larger

Figure 6-19 Use of rear-lit vertical signage and a rear-lit sign simulating stained glass give both retailers distinctive, attractive identities and eliminates headband signage on both stores. Design Director: Robert P. Gersin Associates Inc. Pictures reproduced by permission of the design director.

Figure 6-20 This retailer's interior and exterior signage create the singular decor while conforming to interior store signage criteria for the mall. Design Director: Robert P. Gersin Associates Inc. Pictures reproduced by permission of the design director.

will not help make it memorable. Flashy signs might attract the viewer's attention, but do not necessarily inform; in fact, all the viewer might see is the flash. Simple, good design using the identifying symbol will satisfy the viewer, the ordinances, and the store as it will identify and attract, and be attractive.

Figure 6-21 Use of the store's unique signature in repetitive vertical signage eliminates headbands while clearly identifying the retailer. Design Director: Robert P. Gersin Associates Inc. Pictures reproduced by permission of the design director.

Figure 6-22 Another retailer who chose to eliminate headbands by using repetitive verticals also has his distinctive look while conforming to signage restrictions. Design Director: Robert P. Gersin Associates Inc. Pictures reproduced by permission of the design director.

Figure 6-23 The open storefront chosen by this retailer to accomodate different traffic flow patterns left him little room for signs, but the store's signature can be clearly seen on the exterior and interior signage and at left in the vertical repetition. Design Director: Robert P. Gersin Associates Inc. Pictures reproduced by permission of the design director.

chapter 7

Packaging for the Marketplace

FUNCTION OF PACKAGING

A package must contain or hold merchandise, protect it, and communicate a message about its contents and the company marketing the product. The package should also make a product easy to handle, ship, and display. Product protection and communication are, or should be, closely linked. Protection frequently takes the form of total enclosure, thus hiding the contents, which then must be identified. Of course, communication should go well beyond product identification; it must also sell the product, as it is often a company's only sales tool.

Colors can enhance and make objects more appealing. Trademarks serve as useful, functional ingredients in design and identification. But first things first. A good product can survive poor design of package with massive advertising. On the other hand, a weak product cannot be made more successful for long because the package is appealing. If the corporate identification is strong, one bad item can hurt the company's entire image as consumers will shy away from its other products. So, the package can either contribute to sales and profits, or contribute to costs and losses. For these reasons, packaging decisions should not be relegated to the purchasing or manufacturing departments, where packaging would be purchased in much the same way as are nails, paper, and equipment. Purchasing and manufacturing departments buy to satisfy their company's cost and profit interests, but packages must also satisfy prospective customers. Packaging is a marketing cost and usually a long-range one. The product visible only through or by its package is often the key element in advertising, and certainly plays the major role in point-of-purchase display sales.

PRIVATE LABELS AND NATIONAL BRANDS

When mass merchandisers first entered the field of private labels, the design of the package or label was often not considered to any extent. The price, they felt, was sufficiently low to sell the product without advertising or point-of-purchase appeal. If package design was considered at all, it usually ended up as a copy of the best selling nationally branded product for which the private label company hoped to become a substitute. In many instances, in fact, national brands are packaged in the private label (for example, Kraft private labels its products for A&P), reinforcing the retailer's feelings that price, not the product or package, is the selling point.

In 1969, a research report was sponsored by the Point of Purchase Association and conducted by Ralph Head & Affiliates. The common denominator given for first-time purchasers in supermarkets across the country was, in effect, "I bought it because I saw it displayed." A secondary, but strong, influence on these purchasers was that the package looked like other items made by the same manufacturer. According to this survey, this fact reinforces the argument for corporate identification through a unique and pleasant trademark or symbol for both national and private labels, as the package is a motivating factor worthy of consideration.

Private Labels

There are two schools of thought about the use and design of private labels. Some feel that there is danger in designing private labels with a strong overall identification format. They feel that 10 or 12 percent of the store's merchandise, carrying the private label, can seem overpowering. This figure can hold true in supermarkets who have private label cookies, cereals, soaps, paper goods, and so on. This mode of thinking is based on the premise that all these products carrying the same or similar labels would get boring to the customer or make him feel that this label was being pushed to the exclusion of the other brands. The second school of thought feels that a system of unified package design on all its products can help build the store's image and has the added advantage of being a less expensive way of designing the packages. If the name or symbol is the main design element, color coding can be used as an alternative to the overall design system to differentiate among product lines and groupings, thus identifying without overpowering. This might be the middle ground between the two schools of thought, and it still allows the customer to quickly identify the store's private brands.

Both methods have been developed successfully. Pathmark, a Supermarket General Corporation enterprise, has one name and one package design format for its supermarkets, drug stores, gasoline outlets, and private label merchandise. (See Figure 7-1.) Pathmark divisions' private labels are packaged under one strong corporate identity format system. Whether the product is motor oil or cake mixes, health and beauty aids or soap powder, the Pathmark identification design formula is used. It is the opinion of Pathmark and their design consultants that unified branding in both name and graphics on varying products and product lines allows exchange of equities among products. They feel that any drawbacks conceivable in a private label cake mix looking like the private label soap products is outweighted by the total merits of such an identity system. The end results hoped to be realized by this program is a consumer image of multiple merchandising expertise ranging from food to drugs to floor cleaners and apparel. There is a definite packaging and communications economy in going the Pathmark way—their unified package design actually becomes the in-store atmosphere.

The other approach is taken by Caldor, Inc., in its private label program. Caldor does not feel that the company can communicate to the customers through one package design format. The company separates products into family related groupings, such as baby products, hair care products, and cold remedies. Each grouping has a design format of its own, visually differentiating it from the others. The Caldor symbol is used on all private label products but not as the overall design element as is the case with Pathmark.

No matter which design system is chosen, tight quality control is as essential to private label success as it is to any other product. Private labeling can help a chain store create a distinct image, apart from its competitors, as they will not have the private label products. Consumers are

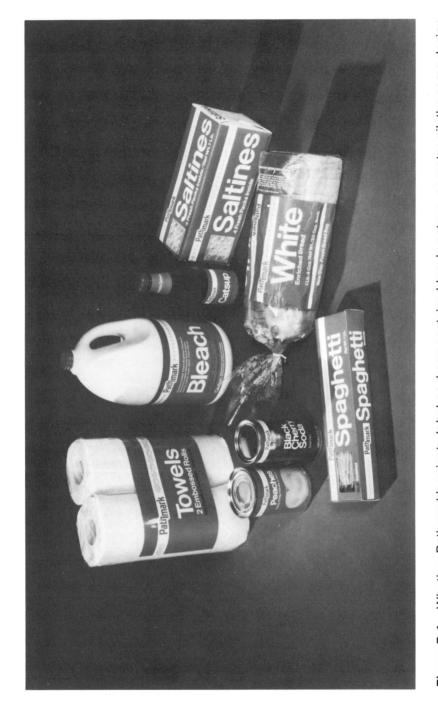

Figure 7-1 Whether Pathmark's private-label package contains bleach, catsup, or motor oil, the same design identification and format is used. Designer: Lippincott and Margulies, Inc.

124

Figure 7-2 Bradlees varies its package design to fit individual product lines, but strongly features the Bradlees symbol as a package design element. Designer: Selame Design Associates.

now accepting private labels as never before; this can be attributed to growing consumer sophistication and concern about prices. If the company has a large enough volume to warrant the expense and design time, it might consider making a re-packaging agreement for a private label of its own with a manufacturer.

National Brands

It is just as important for national brand packaging to be memorable and attractive as it is for private labels, especially with the growing design sophistication of private label products. The discount industry has become the leading general merchandise retailer in the United States, as well as the most important outlet for many nationally branded

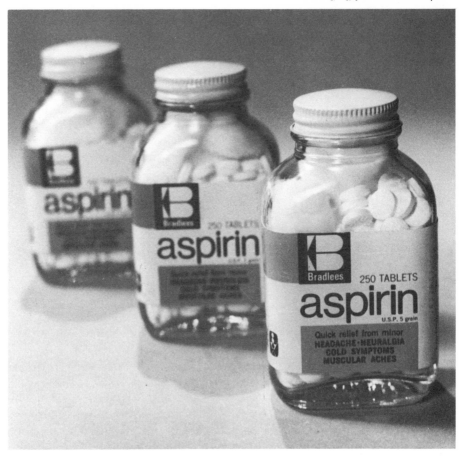

Figure 7-3 Bradlees health and beauty aids carry the company's symbol, as do their paints, but the design format is changed for this category.

products. Even with the upgraded interiors of the discount stores, the merchandise is still piled high to lessen the need for sales personnel in an effort to keep prices low. If the package design is not distinctive, the product will get lost in the crowd of merchandise being offered by the retailer. If the design is not attractive, many pieces together can create an eyesore that will send customers away rather than entice them toward the package. In the growing number of discount stores, especially in the hyper-markets that pile the merchandise to the ceiling, a distinctive, attractive package is a must. The package must attract and then tell the potential purchaser about the contents.

No matter how many sales people a firm has, none of them can know everything about every product. Some of them know little about any product because they are hired to watch the displays or just to keep the stock levels up. In the end, the package and point-of-purchase display must act as the company's best and most informative salesperson.

Figure 7-4A A creative design project for New England Farms takes marketing of the product into careful consideration. This program uniquely provides for point-of-purchase display. The mark is given a prominent position on the package, and the lower wedge color codes the seasonal varieties of potatoes. The large surface on the back of the bag is utilized for communication between the producer and the consumer. Designer: Selame Design Associates.

The text visible on the potato package reads:

The Proper Potato

These Maine potatoes are at their superb best from fall until early summer. These potatoes are especially good for boiling and frying. They are creamy when mashed and crispy when fried.

All our potatoes contain vitamin C, vitamin A, calcium, iron, thiamine, riboflavin, niacin and ascorbic acid which is the reason why it is the most valuable vegetable crop in the world. Potatoes boiled or baked with a low calorie dressing, ketchup or lemon juice can be an invaluable aid to calorie watchers. Although a potato is far more filling than an orange or apple, it contains the same calories.

Empty these potatoes into a bin and store in a cool, moist place away from light.

POTATO RIBBONS

4 large potatoes   Salt and pepper

Pare potatoes and allow to stand wrapped in a towel 10 to 15 minutes to dry thoroughly. Pare round and round each potato to make thick ribbons. Drop each "ribbon" in hot oil. Brown lightly and drain on absorbent paper. Season well. Serves four.

New England Farms
ARLINGTON, MASSACHUSETTS

128

Figure 7-4B   On the back of the New England Farms potato package, a feature entitled "The Proper Potato" tells of its nutritional value, weight watchers hints, little-known facts about seasonal varieties, and recipes. Produce packaging can be a communication medium as well as a protection when handled creatively.

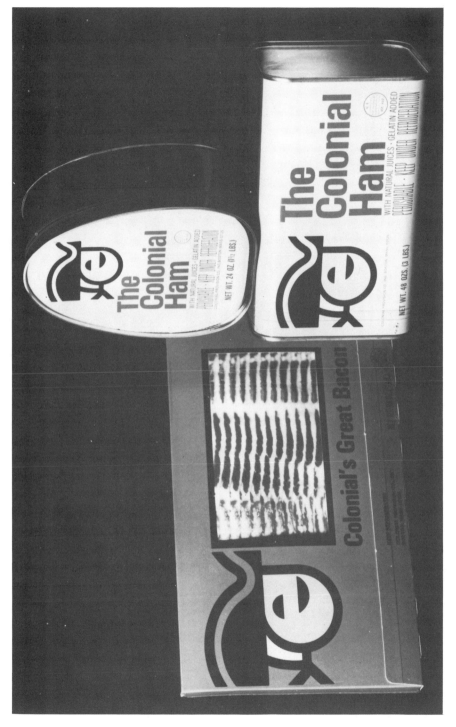

Figure 7-5 Using a symbol strongly on various company product lines provides Colonial Provision Company with the opportunity to market the corporation as well as the individual products. Designer: Selame Design Associates.

Figure 7-6 The prominent symbol on Colonial's packaging also makes their products stand out in the supermarket.

RETAILERS AND MANUFACTURERS MUST BE A TEAM

If the manufacturer understands that he is selling symbols as well as goods, he can view his product more completely. Making a purchase involves assessing the product through the factual and symbolic message it conveys. The symbolic message can encourage the shopper to spend time and money on the purchase or to reject the product and move on. Besides projecting the manufacturer's or private labeler's identity (which, if clearly defined, helps create the symbolic message), the package has to appeal psychologically to the consumer, just as the whole identity must. People do not buy goods only for what they can do, but also for what they mean. A compact economy car gets from one point to another just as well as a Rolls Royce, but the symbolic message of the Rolls Royce will con-

Figure 7-7 Suburbanite identifies its products by displaying its symbol and by following a regulated design format; it also designs its packages for security. Before the design program, an easily pocketed, badly packaged brass brush (left); after, a colorful and tough blister card designed for action sales and stopping palmists (right). Designer: Selame Design Associates.

Figure 7-8 Mops, brushes, and brooms, once thought of as pretty mundane merchandise, are fast becoming part of the most sophisticated merchandising segments on the housewares market. Suburbanite has redesigned its packaging so that its line of cleaning products is easier to shop. Designer: Selame Design Associates.

tinue to make the car a much desired commodity, even though the price of one can buy several smaller cars. When a package is viewed under ordinary shopping conditions, the customer relates not only to its name but also to its size, shape, color, graphic design, and the words on the package. All these elements form our impression of the product in a split second. Packages can talk, and when used properly, can present a strong motivating factor for impulse purchases.

Retailers and manufacturers should work together on packaging and should be equally demanding of each other. The success of any package is also dependent on the physical layout of the display where it is sold. Retailers can be remiss in displaying the package. Packages can be displayed wrong side up or in a sloppy fashion—thrown onto a display. Supermarkets have made great use of the "jumbled display." They throw a large amount of small items, such as cans of vegetables, into a shopping cart or larger container. How can the package attract the customer's eye? The retailing environment in which the package is placed has a great effect on the item's sales. If the atmosphere is annoying or confusing, it will hurt the sales no matter how good the package. Even low-end merchandisers must consider their stores' ambience in their identity programs, thinking of the store itself as the package the consumer sees first.

However, manufacturers are often remiss in their package design. On such things as record cabinets, for example, on some brands the model number is only at one end of the carton. If these are stacked on a shelf, the number may face the back and may not even get unpacked when the shelves are empty. The carton might not even identify the contents as a record cabinet. A progressive manufacturer will put the model number, the name of the piece, and even a line drawing or photograph at both ends. Toy manufacturers are very progressive packagers. Describing and show-ing the contents of the package fully on the outside also prevents the com-mon practice by consumers of opening the package to see what is inside, and then putting the opened box back on the shelf, thereby making that package unsaleable. Having to open the package to see what is inside is also annoying to the customer. The bad image from this annoyance will fall almost equally on the retailer and the manufacturer.

Retailers have to demand good packaging if they expect the products to move well, just as manufacturers have to demand good display if they want their products to move well. If a discounter has set up his store so that the customer does not need sales help except in rare cases, he should not accept a package that does not say what is inside, and so on. The initial time and money spent on good package design will give the manufac-

Figure 7-9   Products are capable of selling a company as much as a company sells the products. Mister Donut revamped its chef with the doughnut in his belly (left) to a more contemporary and protectable mark. Simple designs on packages help build up and retain a quality image (right). Designer: Selame Design Associates.

turer's product and the retailer a good image and will help the retailer to sell the products at a competitive price, as he will need fewer sales people (to everyone's benefit).

In creating package designs for the mass market, it is important to keep the design as simple as possible, but informative. Find the one most important message, present it boldly with very few other competing graphic elements, and visualize the results of the design in a mass display. Does it have strong shelf impact? Will a busy consumer be able to spot the product quickly and easily understand its benefits?

In the need to attract the consumer, sandpaper, lawn tractors, and chocolates do have something in common. More and more, the package must tell its story simply with graphics. People readily understand and remember pictures. The proliferation of facts and details that must now go on packages places a new urgency on telling the main idea clearly and simply. The common thread of all good package design is finding the essence of the product's message, one that is an honest statement about the product, and setting it apart from other like products by presenting that message in a visually and psychologically appealing fashion.

Figure 7-10 When the new symbol is used on packaging, the company is afforded attractive package design for all its private-label products that also reinforces the identity. Designer: Selame Design Associates.

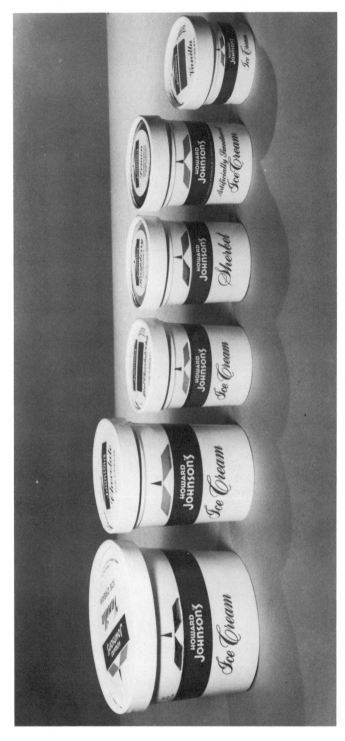

Figure 7-11A　The identification symbol for Howard Johnson's Grocery Products Division appears on a growing line of products available in supermarkets across the country. The basis of the package design is the familiar orange roof and turquoise cupola atop the motor lodge. The name "Howard Johnson's" is in white on a broad turquoise band. Here it appears on the nationally known ice cream package. Designer: Gianninoto Associates, Inc.

136

Figure 7-11B   The Howard Johnson's symbol as it appears on the company's frozen entrees. Designer: Container Corporation of America.

ECOLOGY AND PACKAGING

Businesses should conserve natural resources in the original package, use recyclable materials whenever feasible, or encourage reuse of the package itself. And, they should publicize the fact that their packages can be reused or are made from recycled materials, right on the package itself. In this age of consumerism, openly stating this information will greatly help the image of the manufacturer or the retailer.

Another important point along this vein is the package construction: if it is not convenient or if, once opened, the contents go bad due to poor package design, it will greatly hurt the sales of the item. Many cereal

Figure 7-12   This big red candy apple package provides mouth-watering buying incentive and information at point of purchase for Concord Foods. Designer: Selame Design Associates.

packages are not easy to open, and once opened, the remainder of the contents get stale. Anything detrimental in product or packaging reflects poorly on the corporate image. The packager should publicize improvements in the package with the emphasis on any new protection to the item inside or any reduction in waste of materials or contents. With vocal consumers having a stronger voice in the success or failure of products and businesses, anything that emphasizes resource or price savings is a plus. The package should make these savings clear, stating the facts proudly.

Figure 7-13 Remember that packaging includes carry-out bags and boxes, which should reinforce the store's identity. Kennedy's, a retail clothing chain of Phillips-Van Heusen, projects its store identity as a major design element on their take-home boxes. Designer: Selame Design Associates.

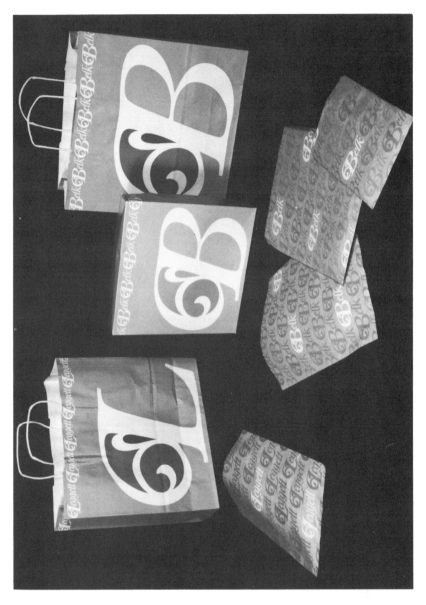

Figure 7-14 A high-fashion signature designed to show the relationship between stores with different names was created for Belk Stores and its affiliates. Blue shopping bags feature a large, stylized initial in white with the store name used to form a border at the top. A repeat motif of the store name in its special script dominates the smaller customer bags, appearing in various colors on the same blue background. Designer: Lippincott & Margulies, Inc.

Figure 7-15 Getting shelf space and attention and retaining them are worth the insurance of top management's personal efforts and the most professional design service available for both private labels and national brands. Designer: Selame Design Associates.

Figure 7-16 Are you able to capture the consumer's attention in the supermarket jungle? When you are up against competition for attention, such as that shown in this photograph, no package design can be left to chance, no matter what type of store it will appear in.

142

SUMMARY

The shirt sleeve merchant will tell you that with enough adver-tising even garbage can be made a desirable household commodity, and with prices spiralling, the shopper is looking for bargains only, not design. However, if a manufacturer or retailer is competing in a low-price line, it still has to distinguish its product bargain from the other product bargains. There could be five brands at exactly the same price. Why do some sell better than others? And, as we have seen in the past several years, the manufacturer and the retailer cannot sell garbage with golden claims and get away with profits for long.

Advertising might get the customers into the store, but good package design sells the products in the store. Good design that makes the identity of the product and manufacturer clear is as important as adver-tising, signage, and store design in attracting and keeping customers. For those retailers who are also manufacturers or who sell their own private label products, the symbol on the package will reinforce the identity, for good or bad. If the package *en masse* becomes ugly, the reinforcement will be bad, and the symbol seen anywhere else will take on a bad connotation. If the package and product are good, the symbol seen anywhere else will take on a positive connotation and promote sales. The importance of good packaging for the marketplace cannot be overemphasized.

chapter 8

Advertising

Not all customers will be interested in every product or store, and they therefore will not be interested in the advertising, either. There is no reason to try to reach everybody. In the initial plans for the identity program, the market to be reached was necessarily pinpointed by the image that the corporation chose and by the merchandise and/or service mix carried. The advertising should aim for the same market with the same identity. In fact, if the corporate identity program has been carefully planned and the merchandise carefully selected, the advertising must reinforce the program and sell the merchandise or all the time and money spent is wasted.

Your advertising and promotion should have a basic verbal and visual message that effectively projects the company's identity, helps create the image, and sells the merchandise, all centering on the corporate symbol. Advertising should not be a self-contained part of the business but an integral part of the total system and corporate identity program because any time that a customer sees the symbol—on a truck, on a package, even on the employees' badges—the company's identity is being reinforced. And, the key to advertising is repetition.

Advertising cannot fulfill its function to the highest degree if everything else the company is doing is not backing up that advertising. The company's basic message has been carefully translated into the components of the identity program and this message should be repeated and kept constant. In a competitive market, the modern advertisement, like the modern package, must do more than attract attention to motivate a purchase. It must give the potential purchaser a reason to buy the product or to shop the store. With so many similar or identical products and stores available, that difference will be the long-range, positive corporate identification. The ads, like the store, must attract, identify, and then merchandise. Many sophisticated companies use their advertising to position the difference between their company and products and those of others, not just to communicate advantages or features. This difference will be reinforced by all advertising using the symbol if the company has clearly defined and projected its identity.

The most important part of such a program is constant and carefully controlled repetition, via all visual expressions put forth by the company. After a period of time, the potential customer will feel familiar with the firm. If someone needs a product or type of store for the first time, he or she will buy the name that is foremost in his memory, and that will be the result of the repetitive advertising. For those who are already customers, advertising can enhance the image.

ADVERTISING WHILE THE PROGRAM IS BEING DEVELOPED

Services necessary to build the retail chain identity are usually outside the scope of the advertising agency. It should be the responsibility of the independent graphic designer in concert with responsible corporate officials to see that these various disciplines are coordinated to create a unified and related total projection of the company's image. However, the people who will do the year-round advertising once the program is formulated should not be kept in the dark. They should be actually involved in the institutional advertising that will introduce the public to the new image as the directives are handed down by the graphic designer. These people should also be asked to give input to the formulation of the program, especially if they also do your market research. The graphic designer has a difficult task when the planning first begins; he not only has to sell his client on his design work for the identity program, he must also sell the people who will do the advertising on the program. If they are not sold, the advertising probably will not meet the standards that the designer sets up.

What's behind
our new symbol?

Figure 8-1A Institutional advertising to introduce the public to a new identity and symbol is important. Andover Bank approached this task with an unusual advertisement. The question and symbol above appeared on one page of the ad.

As the designer and those others responsible set up the specifics of the advertising program, details should be put into the graphic manual to maintain the standards. This includes information available on the way the ads should look and the technical aspects of the advertisements in different media. Once the advertising people have these specifics and the program is underway, they should use the standardized instructions and their creativity within the bounds set up by the "do's" and "dont's" of the graphic manual to create ads that look like they are truthful in every claim

People you can bank on.

Our entire staff is ready, willing and specially trained to help you with all your banking needs.

We're here to answer questions, make suggestions, solve problems.

So, whether you want to open a savings account, apply for a loan, or learn about many other services we offer, look for the symbol. And the people behind it.

Andover Savings Bank, **Andover,** 61 Main St., 475-6103.
N. Andover, 108 Main St., 683-4001. **Methuen,** 547 Broadway. 686-6835

Figure 8-1B The answer and additional message appeared a few pages later. Symbol Designer: Selame Design Associates. Advertisement Designer: Arnold & Company.

Change for a Nickel.

The Boston Five Cents Savings Bank
Ten School Street, Boston 02108

Figure 8-2 Another institutional advertisement introducing a new symbol takes a different, but equally effective, approach. Symbol Designer: Selame Design Associates. Advertisement Designer: Arnold & Company.

(and, of course, they should be—nothing is worse for an image than false advertising) and that easily reflect that the product being sold belongs to the company. The second requirement will be facilitated by a uniform corporate image and a well-written graphic manual. They should do this advertising to those people in the market that the identity program has chosen to reach.

If the advertising agency does not follow the guidelines voluntarily, demand their compliance or switch to another agency. There is no sense in working with (or against) an offended artist while watching the effort behind the program's implementation go down the drain. The collaboration between graphic designer and ad agency is more important after the implementation than before or during, but if the relationship is not set up at the beginning the company might run into trouble. This is why the designer has to sell the program to the agency; by including them in the initial planning, the selling job will be made easier.

When American Motors revamped their identity, they felt that one of the most innovative aspects of the identification program was the interior design of their dealerships. In order to tie the showrooms in to advertising to stress this innovation, they studied the possibility of playing the same music in their showrooms as they did in the advertisements. In this way, the company's visual communications are also reinforced audibly, and so create a strong method of reinforcing the identity.

The relationship of the advertising agency to American Motors was a very strong one. It was also considered to be a major factor in the company's sales turnaround. Once the agency agreed to sign the news ads and other print material with the company's new symbol, the project director felt he had a major endorsement and the cooperation that was needed if the program was to work as intended.

DAY-TO-DAY ADVERTISING WITH THE NEW IDENTITY

Once the entire program is implemented and the advertising agency is back in full control of advertising, the coordination of the day-to-day advertising with the new identity must begin. Up until now, the new symbol would have, or should have appeared in institutional ads that let the public know the company was changing its appearance. The trademark or symbol is the link between all the company's advertising and promotional efforts and the company, and it must be used strategically in all advertising and promotion.

Once the identity plan is constructed and approved, it is the time for the agency and the internal staff to start the new program. The staff should be taught the important "what to do's" or "what not to do's," and these should be clearly laid out in the graphic manual.

The advertising agency is rarely called upon to analyze a retail chain's total communications picture and procedures. They are usually involved, justifiably, in the everyday advertisement decisions, which can often limit the quality of coordination among the advertisements in all media and between the media and the company's other visual matter. The corporate identity program, to be successful, needs this coordination.

The media advertising dollar is usually broken down this way: the largest amount, 36 percent, goes to newspapers; 25 percent goes to radio and television broadcasts; and 13 percent goes to direct mail. As the corporate identity is all visual, some might think that the radio could not work well in the advertising campaigns. However, if properly coordinated by the same agency, the radio ads could also be tied in by using the tag lines of the printed and television ads, or even by a description of the symbol. We have all heard advertisements for many companies that end, "Remember, look for the . . ." and then a description of the easily identifiable symbol. Using one coordinator allows the advertising to also be positioned the same: getting at the same market, picking the correct hours and stations and channels to reach the highest percentage of people tuned in from the chosen segments, and so on.

There is really no substitute for objective analysis by those experienced in corporate identity when planning the day-to-day ads. These professionals have no preconceived opinions of the best course of action for the company—they do not prefer one communication medium over any other. They realize from their experience that the total visual image adds up to the total communications. The company will gain the benefit of years of experience and accomplishments with varied corporate and store and product identification problems. To work, the client has to trust that he has chosen the graphic designer well and has to be flexible and open to surprises in all facets of the design including the ad suggestions regarding places of ads and positioning.

The size of the identifying symbol or package appearing in a television commercial or a newspaper ad is usually proportional to how much the creative people at the agency like or dislike the design. To prevent the symbol from disappearing, its specifics not only have to appear in the manual but the agency has to be sold on the program. This, again, is the main reason to include them in the planning.

collect a classic summer look:
the barnsville dress

$26

Treat yourself to classic lines and the easy care that
Barnsville texturized polyester knits are known
for. Barnsville dresses keep their shape, resist wrinkles,
pack and unpack with the greatest of ease. Easy to
care for at home or abroad, they're hand or
machine washable, drip or machine dry and need
no ironing. Choose brown or
burgundy in the styles shown,
sizes 8 to 18.
kennedy's — misses' dresses

it's the blazer . . .

the year's biggest news from kennedy's

Figure 8-3 When Kennedy's changed its look and symbol, they were aim-
ing at a younger clientele. The old look (above) attracted an older, more con-
servative customer. The new ad (below) follows the same basic format, but
the new symbol changes the whole look of the ad. Symbol Designer: Selame
Design Associates. Advertisement Designer: Kennedy's Staff.

152

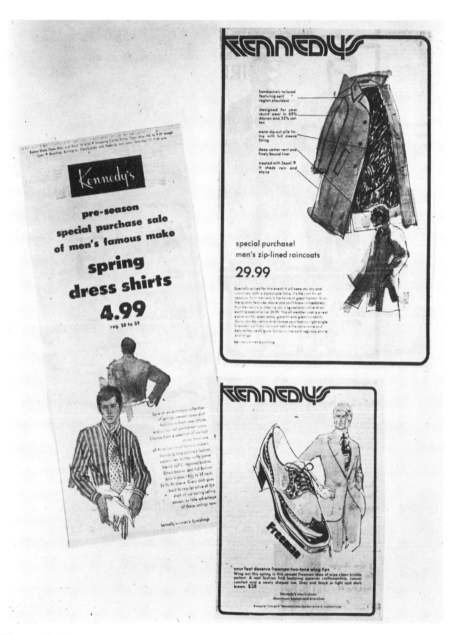

Figure 8-4   The Kennedy's ad for men's wear went through the same change, the whole look being modified with the use of the image-building symbol.

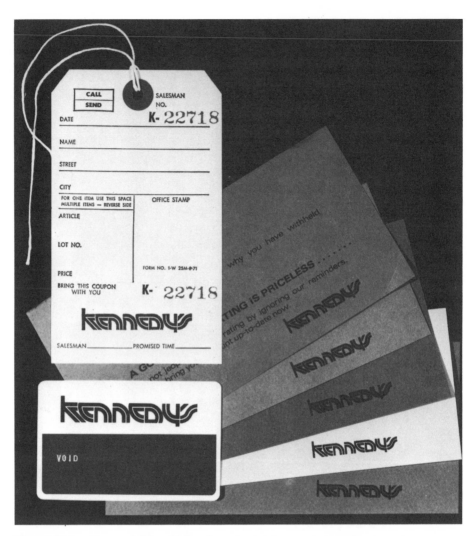

Figure 8-5 Kennedy's collateral material is now organized and contemporary looking, also through the use of the symbol. Any material on which the signature appears serves as further advertising for the company. Designer: Selame Design Associates.

Again, familiarity is the key to advertising effectiveness. Even though messages need to change from one medium to the next and from week to week, a format concept should be planned, which, of course, should always use the image-building symbol. Strong integration among the various media advertisements gives a company more mileage from its advertising dollars. (See Figure 8-5.)

With advertising volume due to increase by 65 percent in the next decade, with the proliferation of options on how to spend money increasing every year, the advertiser is facing a multiplicity of choices that can be either an exciting challenge or turn into a serious problem. And remember, no one will get his money back if the ad is not good. The increasing costs make getting the most for the money essential. It makes it important to make as few different commercial statements as possible and to provide a thread of continuity from one commercial to the next. And because of these rising costs, it may pay to spend some money on thorough research to determine which medium at which time and to which area will give you the lowest cost and most impressive advertising, always judging the cost on the per capita cost of the ad. The money saved and the mileage gained might more than make up for the expense of the research.

A person watching television six hours a day will be exposed to 90 commercials per day. The more he sees consecutively, the more he will not remember. Someone watching a sequence of five consecutive commercials will remember the first one the best (and this is why this position is more expensive), and then attention drops off after the initial period and continues to decline. The opening sequence of any commercial is therefore very important as the ad must capture and hold the attention of viewers to prevent them from mentally or physically tuning out. (See Figure 8-6.) This first impression is important in all facets of the identity program; in fact, the importance of the first visual impression can even be thought of as the reason for starting an identity program.

The average consumer is exposed to a minimum of 560 advertising messages a day, 484 of which he completely blocks out. Bold symbols can help prevent the viewer from blocking out the ad in any advertising medium and will help identify the sponsor of the ad at the same time.

MAKE THE MOST OF POTENTIAL ADVERTISING SPACE

Because they are often handicapped by small advertising budgets, many retailers need to review the efficiency of their advertising and to look for ways to stretch their precious advertising and promotion dollars. A strong symbol and a corporate identity program that has reached every area of the company can be the answer.

There are visual media available to all where they can advertise their companies and products at no extra cost. For example, the trucks, company cars, and other rolling stock are not any more expensive to buy

Figure 8-6 The opening sequence of any television commercial must hold the viewer's attention or he will tune out. The Stop & Shop Companies used to open their ads with an animated formation of their symbol, creating interest and recognition. Designer: Selame Design Associates.

and run when they are attention getters and environmental assets than are the tired looking vehicles that go unnoticed on our highways.(See Figure 8-7.) This is a great untapped source of free advertising when they are fitted with trademarks or symbols.

Packaging, sales promotion, and signage all cost money for materials. If they do not help to actually advertise the company's products or store, then they are not adding to sales and might just as well be plain to save the printing expenses. Symbols that can become focal promotional tools, whether on trucks, company uniforms, packages, signs, or even clothing, allow the business to effectively communicate a sales message even with a limited budget.

Figure 8-7A Goren Food Company in New Jersey is an example of how simple graphics and strong colors create a visually unique and appealing identifying symbol on trucks as well as on other media. Goren's was very strong in its own market. However, when sold to Norris Grain Company in Chicago, the advent of geographical and product growth was apparent. It had to look its expanded part to compete successfully with Carnation and Campbell Soups; it needed to look contemporary and national. The trucks before the program very likely went unnoticed on the road.

For instance, Wechsler Coffee Corporation, a division of Restaurant Associates, wanted to unify the rapidly acquired divisional names, which were beginning to confuse even Wechsler's prime customers, so they initiated a corporate identity program. The new symbol, the Wechsler "W," is uniquely used repetitively to create the striking design across their vehicles. (See Figure 8-9.) The design concentration of the chocolate brown band across the bottom of the vehicle is also an effective factor in maintaining clean looking trucks, as the dark color in this dust-collecting and splash-prone area tends to hide the dirt accumulated on trips. The white background on the rest of the vehicle not only looks clean but also serves as a striking contrast to the magenta symbol.

Trademarks are in Fashion

Trademarks can even be fashionable, providing great promotion and publicity. The designer signature scarves that have gained great pop-

Figure 8-7B   Once they were redesigned, Goren's trucks' large expanse of corporate symbol, slogan, and color scheme created a highly visible and appealing advertisement for this company. The symbol is in red and gold on a black vinyl background flanked by two red panels. The corporate signature is in white precut vinyl. Designer: Selame Design Associates.

ularity over the past few years are a most common example of how to advertise the company's products on the products themselves, without being offensive or overbearing. The signature bags of Louis Vuitton are another example; and these bags are priced so that only the affluent can afford them. The "LV" in its distinctive pattern has become quite a status symbol in many areas of the country as well as abroad.

There are other uses for symbols or trademarks in fashions besides imposing these on the company's products themselves. Goodwill Industries is now using symbol fashions as part of its own fashion shows. (See Figure 8-10.) The dresses, coats, and pantsuits carrying the Goodwill mark are designed by Schjelde of Boston (under the supervision of Selame Design) as well as by the women who run the show. A company can also

Figure 8-8 When the corporate symbol is used on rolling stock, the business can communicate a sales message and image even with a limited budget. Alperts uses the same symbol and signature on its trucks as it uses on storefronts, creating an attractive, unified look. Designer: Selame Design Associates.

use symbol fashions for models to wear at store openings, for sales employees' uniforms, and as attention-getters on television commercials. If the outfits are stylish enough, customers might even want them for their own wardrobes (another no-extra-cost advertising medium); it *has* happened.

According to the first apparel market research study made by Fross & Sullivan, Inc., the annual career apparel market will climb to almost $300 million by 1981 from the current volume of $65 million. The study also predicts that career apparel, which differs from uniforms by its fashionable styling, individuality, and use in white-collar jobs, will expand to cover more job categories.

SUMMARY

The importance of analyzing the market to be reached is essential in advertising successfully at the best price, but that is true for any company with or without a corporate identity program. Those with identity programs with strong symbols, however, have the advantage of ready-made repetition in their symbols. If implemented properly, the corporate

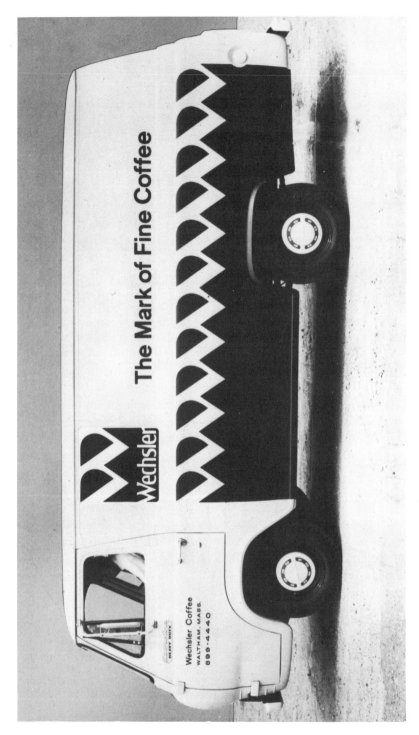

Figure 8-9 Wechsler makes use of its symbol and bold colors, key ingredients to visibility and recall, on their company trucks. They realize that words alone on fast-moving vehicles will not get a message across to the viewer. Designer: Selame Design Associates.

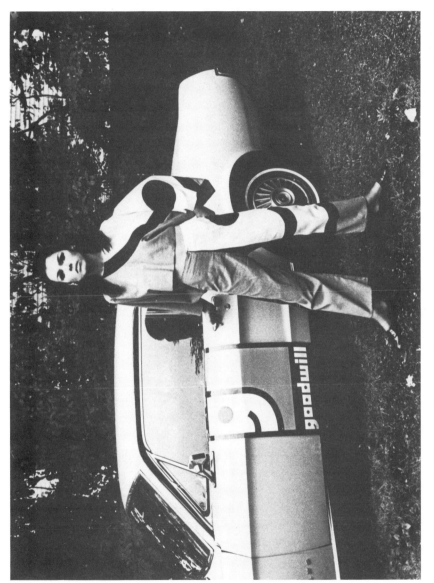

Figure 8-10 Goodwill Industries uses its symbol on clothing for its fashion shows as well as on its other visual material, including the company car shown above. Designer: Schjelde.

Figure 8-11   The Bradlees symbol has been turned on its side to create the shape as well as the colors of this fashion outfit. Designer: Schjelde and Selame Design Associates.

162

Figure 8-12 Brigham's symbol inspired this dress, which can be worn anywhere, creating further advertising for the company. Designer: Schjelde and Selame Design Associates.

Figure 8-13   This bright and attractive casual summer dress was designed from the Stop & Shop symbol. Designer: Schjelde and Selame Design Associates.

Figure 8-14 Pearlridge Mall's symbol makes an interesting pattern on this top that could easily be sold with pride alongside any manufacturer's line. Design Director: Robert P. Gersin Associates Inc. Picture reproduced by permission of the design director.

identity program allows the company to advertise at no extra cost in many areas—on trucks, signs, packages, and even fashions—with the help of the symbol. It is essential that the corporate designer and those who do the company's advertising work together from the beginning in order to create successful institutional advertising to let the public know about the upcoming change in appearance and then later to put into effect a successful, integrated advertising program that will give the firm the greatest effective exposure at the least cost.

chapter 9

International Marketing and Identity

Once the company has decided what it has and what it is that other countries want, how does it go about supplying that want? Does it take the operation intact and operate the same way all over the world? Of course, if that could be done successfully, international marketing would be an easy, enjoyable experience. It is not really easy, but it should be profitable and interesting. However, some companies are faced with problems before the welcome mats are set out. To avoid immediate problems and possible exclusion from other countries, the company should make sure that it is dressed well enough to go visiting.

In these times of bad feelings among so many nations, take-overs of American companies by the governments of the countries where the branches are located, and emergence of new countries onto the international marketing scene, small- and medium-sized companies should not assume that the international market is not for them. Their size might be their key to success if they capitalize on their personal approach to the consumer. The reasons for success and failure in other countries, barring political upheavals that affect everyone, are similar to those for success and failure in the United States. If the company's image is favorable, it will be accepted. A weak image or one that portrays contempt or indifference toward consumers will eventually show up on the books in red ink.

An analysis of the potential market and the competition in any country should of course be made, but that is not in the scope of this book. That survey and the decision to go international is the first step; checking the legal procedures involved is the second; and then it is time to look into how the company's identity and image fit into the customs and marketing climate in the countries slated for expansion.

If the company decides to merge with a foreign company or to hire nationals to run its foreign branches, it will have a built-in staff of experts to guide it toward local acceptance. If not, thorough research must be done in all areas of operations and social interaction by someone in the company or by a hired consultant.

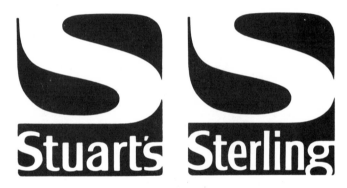

Figure 9-1 Wechsler's affiliates in Canada—Stuart's Branded Coffee Ltd. and Sterling Teas & Coffee Ltd.—are shown to be part of the Wechsler family by creating the symbols from the same typography and color scheme, unifying the international look but retaining the separate company names. Designer: Selame Design Associates.

TRADEMARKS, SYMBOLS, AND COMPANY NAMES

If the company considered the possibility of going international before starting its identity program, the trademark and symbol were probably checked for international acceptance. If not, some research is called for. A trademark search similar to that made for United States clearance must be made in foreign countries. In those countries that operate under a common-law legal system, the first company to use a mark owns it. In those countries that follow civil law, the first to register the mark

Figure 9-2 In Japan, western culture is popular and so very little change was necessary in the foreign Mister Donut shop exterior.

Figure 9-3 One very real difference, however, is the scarcity of land in Japan. When Mister Donut of America built the first few prototypes, they were based on the same ground floor square footage as in the United States, but adjustments were made to use vertical rather than horizontal space. The office area, once on the ground level, is now a small, second-floor addition.

in that country owns it. It is therefore advisable to register a mark as soon as the company decides to open in a foreign country.

Once the mark and/or symbol have been cleared, the firm must make sure that the colors, name, and picture are not comical, offensive, disrespectful, or even obscene in the foreign nation. In bi-lingual countries, it must be checked out in all languages. A well-planned and visually appealing mark in the United States could be the ruin of a company in another country. To use an extreme example, "Elsie," the Borden cow, would hardly sell any cheese or milk in India, where cows are considered sacred. In fact, she would probably have the population in an uproar.

If everything is clear up to this point, the company should make

Figure 9-4 Creative Japanese franchisees developed a uniform based on the Mister Donut signature. Caps carry the mark, uniforms the signature. Creative thinking from foreign branches can often be used to upgrade the entire company.

one more decision. Should any printing that appears on the trademark and symbol appear in the original English, or should it be transliterated or even translated into the language of the local population? The location of the outlet might influence this decision. In most big cities around the world, there is no harm in advertising that the firm is American and proudly displaying the English lettering. In some smaller towns or off the beaten track, the feelings of the nationals towards Americans should be considered. If there is any question, it might be best not to use English too often. As in the United States, the first impression of any company is the most important one, so the face displayed to the world should be carefully considered.

ごあいさつ

合掌

暑さ厳しき折、いかがお過ごしてございましょう。さて、私どもの新事業のひとつとして、昨年来より手掛けてまいりましたミスタードーナツ。その〈第1号箕面パイロットショップ〉の開店に当たりましては、あなたさまにひとかたならぬお力添え、またお引立てを賜り、厚くお礼申し上げます。おかげさまて当ショップも、予想以上の好成績をおさめ、数知れぬお客さまに私たちのまごころをお届けすることができました。事業部一同、心から感謝いたしております。さらに、加盟店募集活動も着実に軌道に乗り、この9月にはミスタードーナツ大学ともいうべき〈研修センター〉か江坂に設立されることとなりました。

つきましては、この〈損の道をゆく〉今月号は、これまでの私たちの活動経過を、まとめてごらんいただきたいと〈ミスタードーナツ特集〉を組みました。どうぞごらんくださいませ。

今後ともよろしくお引立て、また心あるご進言を賜りますよう、お願い申し上げます。

合掌

株式会社ダスキン ミスタードーナツ事業部

Figure 9-5 The peripheral communication materials of the international branches can also be patterened after those of the home branch. The Mister Donut Japanese stationery is distinguishable from its U.S. counterpart only by the Japanese writing.

ARCHITECTURE AND SIGNAGE

The United States is not the only country with protective and restrictive ordinances for architecture and signage. In fact, the laws in this area can be even stricter in foreign countries than here. The architect and lawyer should study the laws carefully to determine whether or not the firm has to make a major overhaul in its design program in this area.

Again, it is basically a matter of checking into the local customs, likes and dislikes. In countries such as France that have grown accustomed to the hypermarches, a large store would not turn any heads. In smaller, less-developed countries, however, a 200,000 square foot unit would probably frighten off more customers than it attracted. Many people would also be outraged at the effect on the environment if a large, American store was built in the middle of an area that formerly held only small shops surrounded by rolling countryside. There are also subtle differences that have to be studied before erecting any structure in any country.

It is also not only a question of whether or not the building and signage are legal. The image the firm portrays is more important to the profits of the company than the size and colors of the structures. The Singer Company is committed to the international market place philosophically as well as financially. For example, in Turkey Singer agents set up retail centers on market day, fitting their operation into the shopping habits of the citizens. In Thailand, Singer owns and operates boats as floating shops. (See Figure 9-6.) By operating this way, Singer not only portrays its proud identity, but finds ways of fitting into the local scene, improving its image.

So, rigid adherence to the design program set up for the United States operation, where it has proven successful, does not assure success abroad. The firm can keep the trademark, the symbol, and the name but still might find it more profitable to change the entire look of the architecture and signage.

PACKAGING AND ADVERTISING

As with any other aspect of international marketing, the packaging and advertising might have to depart from the basic design to sell the company abroad. There are also laws in other countries that might make it necessary to change the firm's advertising approach.

For example, if in Germany the firm advertises that its product is

Figure 9-6 Singer fits its merchandising techniques to the locale but retains its proud identity. In Singapore the company uses boats to transport its products to the marketplace. Picture reproduced by permission.

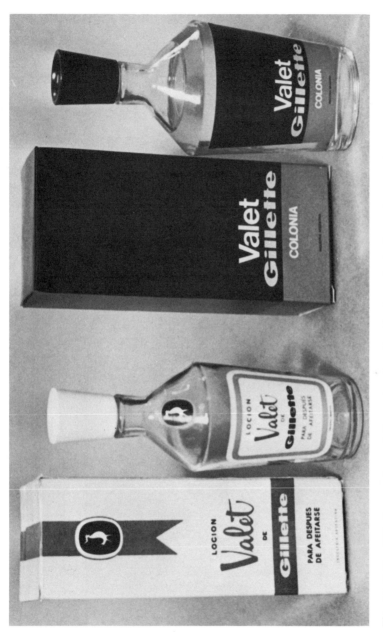

Figure 9-7 Gillette packaged its entry for South America's lucrative men's cologne market in a package similar to its U.S. counterpart. After a disappointing sales picture with Valet in its old packaging, Gillette realized that the men of South America were more sophisticated in their use of cologne and would spend more for it. The new package design reflected this sophisticated market. Designer: Selame Design Associates.

Figure 9-8 A second product entry, Valet Shampoo, capitalized on the equity of the Gillette name that was being established in the South and Central American markets. The shampoo package was designed to attract the entire family. It also serves as an aid to retail display, as it allows the tubed product to stand up. The cartons are utilized for graphic explanations. The sides have a line drawing of a family to show that it is for either sex and all ages. The back has contents and other information. This is a Guillette International product and is sold only in foreign countries. Designer: Selame Design Associates.

176

PUBLISHER'S ERRATA SHEET

The Publisher draws the reader's attention to the
following errata in this text:

The designer of the Safeway symbol depicted
on page 177 should read Cornelius Sampson &
Associates of San Francisco rather than Walter
Landor Associates.

The Publisher apologizes for this error which will be
corrected at reprint.

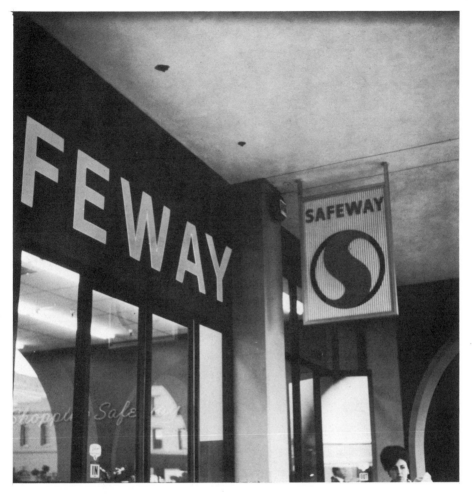

Figure 9-9   The Safeway sign and symbol as it appears in the United States, here in San Fransisco, California. Designer: Walter Landor Associates.

the best, it can be sued for slander by a competitor. Japanese advertisers claiming that their product is the best or that it sells the most have to be prepared to back up these claims with hard data proving the contentions.

Labeling laws in other countries also need checking. There are laws stating what information has to appear on the package, and often the law calls for more information than that currently required in the United States. But here again, customer acceptance is the name of the game. What is attractive to people in the particular country of sale should determine the

Figure 9-10 The printing on a Safeway shopping bag used in England reflects the same symbol, both for the bag itself and on the packages shown on the bag. At times, there is no need to change any part of the visual identity.

shape, size, and color of the package. (See Figures 9-7 and 9-8.) The company should keep its trademark in order to keep its identity, but change the look of the package if necessary. After a time of customer acceptance, it might be possible to revert to the packaging used in the United States, as long as the trademark lets the customers know that the producer has not changed.

SUMMARY

The center of the identity program, the trademark/symbol, can make or break the international marketing success of any company. If the mark has been well designed and can easily be recognized by any person of any background who speaks any language, the chances for foreign success are greatly enhanced. Although the symbol should remain constant to carry through the identity program, the other aspects of the design program might need modification to better suit the tastes, customs, and laws of foreign countries.

Careful research into these aspects must be made, and the company should leave itself open to suggestions once it has started its foreign marketing program. People in the foreign branches often make innovative suggestions that will improve the profitability of those branches. The parent company should listen to these suggestions, as the people on the scene get to know what their customers want and what they respond to.

The identity manual should reflect these foreign programs, and carry the same detailed information for every aspect of the foreign design as they carry for the U.S. program. If the firm has hired nationals to work in the overseas branches, it might be a good idea to print the manual in their own language to make sure the details are understood and carried through. Sharing this information in every branch can allow each office to gain from the experience of every other office, and possibly leave the door open for the creative thinking that sets the innovators apart from the crowd.

chapter 10

The Corporate Identity Manual

Once you have put it all together, how do you keep it that way? The key to any program's success, as we have already emphasized, lies in constant control to ensure adherence to the program. This follow-through depends on the strength of the corporate identity director, and he in turn relies on the corporate identity manual.

An identification program is never really finished. It must be adapted to growth and changes in the company, in the prevailing business climate, in fashions, and in social mores. A strong identity program should be able to bridge the years successfully. Using the manual ensures that standards established by the design consultant and agreed upon by management are consistently upheld. When changes or additions are needed, and the executives' agreement has been given, they are incorporated into the manual to keep it up to date and complete. In this way, the manual continues to be the official guideline for every aspect of the program.

WHAT GOES INTO AN IDENTITY MANUAL?

There is one word that can describe what goes into the identity manual: *everything*. The Corporate Identification Checklist in Chapter 2 shows the numerous items affected by the company's program. For any of these items, there should be an entry in the manual. This entry should include:

1. Proper use of the item.
2. How the item is designed to fit into the program.
    a. Color (be specific; include paints and inks, with brands and numbers if possible)
    b. Size(s)
    c. Typeface used
    d. Position of symbol and typeface on item
    e. Any variations allowed in color, typeface, size, position
3. Where the item can be ordered (if one or a few places are used for all parts of the company.)

Of course, any area that is not on the checklist but is designed to fit into the program should also be included in the manual.

The manual should be easy to read, understand, and follow. Straight textual matter should be kept to a minimum, being replaced by lists and illustrations whenever possible. Each item or topic should be preceeded by a headline so that it can be found easily. A table of contents or index is important.

No matter how the text is handled, two things should always be included:

1. A statement at the beginning of the text saying that any situation not covered in the manual is to be discussed with the corporate identity director and agreed upon before its implementation.
2. A short explanation of why the company has initiated the program, what it hopes the program will achieve, and the rewards the program will give to the individual as well as to the company. Also stress here the importance of following the manual exactly and using the trademark and symbol properly.

Reproduction Art for Symbols

If the advertising or material for the company is not purchased by headquarters or one supplier is not convenient for all parts of the company, there should be some way of assuring that all symbols will look the same. The easiest and most efficient method of doing this is to provide several copies of each size symbol in each manual. These copies should be in a form that allows direct reproduction. If complicated processes are involved in the reproduction, such as screens or tints, complete instructions for each type should be given as well.

For example, if the company's symbol is all linework, it should be provided on a good 70 pound coated text stock, and should be shown in diminishing sizes from 3 inches down to ¼ inch and numbered for reference. The art itself must be clear and sharp. If it is color, the copies should show the exact colors reproduced on coated (glossy) stock and on uncoated (flat) stock in order to show the supplier what to match, depending on the stock to be used. The color sample pages are sometimes perforated with a self-adhesive backing to make it easy to apply color swatches to artwork going to the supplier.

There are many technicalities involved in reproducing art, and many more than those just given for including copies in the manual. For this reason, the design consultant should oversee at least this part of the manual so that he can advise management on these technical areas. The important point is that the symbols provided should be exact in every way and provided in a form ready for reproduction. Otherwise, slight variations will start appearing; these slight variations will get larger; and the whole effort will have been wasted.

The importance of artwork to the whole program should be obvious. The emphasis on art in Howard Johnson's identity manual can be seen in the following excerpts from their manual. This company has always felt that its art was of central importance to its program; in fact, it has been rumored that color chips were placed in a vault for safe-keeping!

In one of their early manuals, the company stressed the successful standardization of identification elements. They achieved this by means of master drawings that were continually photoprinted for use on final art.

This was a satisfactory control because Alcott Associates (the designers) either executed or directed the execution of all Howard Johnson package designs.

Color standards were effectively maintained by means of the attached visual controls in the manual. Although inks respond differently to various stocks and printing processes making an identical match impossible, it is possible to produce colors on any white stock that fall within the visual tolerances, which the company adhered to strictly.

As an example, in the case of orange, it is very easy to observe whether a proposed match is too red, too yellow, too light or too dark. Even though a color is not an identical match with the center color, it is a commercially acceptable match if it falls within the tolerance limitations.

Pages from the company's recent manual, designed by Gianninoto Associates, Inc. are reproduced on the following pages.

REPRODUCTION ART

For reproduction, use only authorized reproduction copies of the original Trademarks and logotypes, in various sizes, enclosed at the back of this manual.

TRADEMARK-LOGOTYPE VERSIONS

Only the trademark-logotype versions designated in this manual are authorized. Do not reproduce the trademark-logotype in outline, in linear enclosures, or with a border. No portion of the trademark-logo should be cropped or cut for any reason.

The complete logotype may be embossed (raised from the surface), but never debossed (depressed into the surface).

COLOR

The Howard Johnson's Standard Orange and Turquoise are an integral part of the company's image. Among the following pages are descriptions of the way these colors should be reproduced in the trademark.

At the back of this manual are accurate color swatches depicting the Howard Johnson's Standard Orange and Turquoise on —

UNCOATED PAPER

COATED PAPER

ONE COLOR PRINTING

Since both the Orange and Turquoise are an integral part of the
Howard Johnson's image, one-color printing should be avoided
whenever possible. The following information will apply to
newspaper ads and other situations where one-color printing is
unavoidable.

Black and Tone Treatment

When printing is restricted to only black ink, the roof
segment of the trademark (cupola not included) should be
screened. When line-screens other than the 120 line and
60 line-screens shown here are used, match the tone
(darkness) of the gray roof to the tone of the gray roof in the
"Correct" illustrations below.

CORRECT TONE: 120 line screen

CORRECT TONE: 60 line screen

INCORRECT: Gray tone too dark

INCORRECT: Gray tone too light

One Color (Other Than Black)

Where printing is restricted to one color *other than black*,

the roof segment of that color should *not be screened*,

making the entire trademark appear in a solid color. Again,

THIS SITUATION SHOULD BE AVOIDED WHENEVER

POSSIBLE!

Reverse Printing

If, for any reason, the trademark is used in reverse, as

depicted below, no screens are used. Any of the supplied

trademarks in this manual may be used as art and reversed

by the engraver.

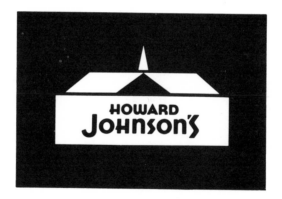

Include "Don'ts"

The danger of using any trademark or symbol improperly can never be overlooked, either from a legal or identity viewpoint. A helpful way to avoid the improper use of any item is to include several examples of what constitutes improper use of the item following the explanation of the proper method of display. This not only underlines the correct use but also will emphasize that the design was carefully constructed for a reason and any variation on that design will detract from the program.

The following excerpts from the American Motors manual, designed by Lippincott & Margulies, Inc., are good examples of how to illustrate the "don'ts."

Since the corporate identification system relies heavily upon simple, clear visual statements, the corporate signature should always stand as a separate entity. It is important that it be easily seen and understood at a glance and, therefore, it must never be confused by the close proximity of distracting design elements.

Never use a drop-shadow.

Never position signature with distracting elements.

Never enclose signature in a shape.

Basic Usage

1/13   **Reproduction Control**

American Motors

Sharp, clear and undistorted reproduction quality is important in order to ensure a consistent appearance of the corporate signature.

Reproduction should be made only from officially designated reproduction sheets which appear in the back of this manual.

American Motors

Never allow distortion.

American Motors

Never allow too heavy an impression.

American Motors ◥▮

Never allow the signature to be out of focus.

Architecture and Signage

In Chapters 5 and 6, we discussed the design considerations involved in interior and exterior architecture and signage. These aspects might not involve any work by different stores in a chain or by different branches of a company if the headquarters staff oversees these operations. If this is the case, then a section in the manual covering this part of the identity program is not essential for store or branch managers. It might be desirable to include so they can be aware of the areas under the program's control or if they are expected to make sure that everything is properly maintained.

When store-level people do get involved, as would be the case with several franchised chains or with subsidiaries owned but not operated by the parent company (among others), architecture and signage control sheets must be included in every copy of the manual. These pages, like those for any other item in the manual, are used for supplier specifications and bids. Once the standards are set, several operators can get together to take advantage of quantity discounts as they will all be ordering the same signs or material.

The following pages are excerpted from the first American Motors manual, designed by Lippincott & Margulies, Inc. Prior to this identity program, the parent company had not set many restrictions on its dealerships' architecture and signage, so the directions to the dealers are quite complete. However, the manual also explains the reason for each step of the program so that the sudden controls are acceptable, reasonable, and desirable. This tone is the ideal for any manual.

A Plan of Action

We recognize that each of our more than 2,300 dealerships is different from the rest. However, because the new Dealership Facility Identification System has been created around an extremely flexible design plan, it can be adapted to every American Motors Dealership regardless of size, current layout or architectural style.

To meet this challenge, American Motors Corporation, through its Office of Corporate Identity, has developed a positive plan of action that will help you to upgrade your individual dealership so that it will be similar in appearance to the Grosse Pointe prototype.

In the weeks and months ahead you will receive specific recommendations as to how and when each aspect of the new Dealership Facility Identification System will be implemented. For example, guidelines will be issued for the:

changeover in signage,
painting of facilities,
installation of approved lighting and flooring,
construction of closing offices and customer write-up desks, and
application of graphics.

At the appropriate time, specifications, schedules, construction diagrams and other pertinent source information will be forwarded to you.

Total program recommendations will be sent in the form of a Dealership Facilities Manual of loose-leaf design. This will outline basic procedures and detail creative actions every dealer can take to become an integral part of this sales-stimulating program. Specific information contained in subsequent mailings can be inserted for handy reference.

Caution: Do not proceed with any aspects of this program, such as ordering paint or signs, until you receive detailed instructions.

Exterior Design

Because of the many different types of architectural styles exhibited by the company's numerous dealership facilities, deliberate architectural understaging was called for. Our purpose in this was to "un-design" the Grosse Pointe building to minimize colors and shapes in such a way that a consistent format could be developed and applied uniformly to all existing facilities in our dealership network. With this thought in mind, let's take a closer look at the prototype facility.

Building Identification

Exterior of the Grosse Pointe building has been un-designed by application of neutral paint colors. The purpose of this is to create an effective background for the A-mark and the new identification of the dealer's name on the fascia of the building. White lettering against the black field provides for the greatest contrast and legibility.

Primary Identification Sign (Pylon)

Unlike others normally seen in the automobile industry, this sign, or pylon, has more effective sign area because it is vertical and completely solid all the way down to its base. There are several good reasons for this: First, our name is too long to be communicated horizontally with any great degree of effectiveness. Secondly, the A-mark symbol lends itself particularly well to this sort of rectangular treatment. In fact, the very uniqueness of the American Motors pylon topped with the new mark creates an unforgettable point of reference. Again, the combination of black background and white lettering assures maximum legibility. Another point considered by the designers pertained to the fact that today more and more communities are becoming increasingly critical of the garishness and vulgarity of many signs erected by business. The tasteful and modern American Motors pylon will meet even the most stringent community requirements. Also, it is adaptable to different types of mounting devices, including wall mounts.

Service Area Identification

Like the pylon, this sign also runs vertically along the wall by the service area entrance. It is topped by the new mark, and the word "Service" appears in white letters on a solid black field. More adaptable than former service signs, it aids the customer in identifying the service entrance. The repetition of the basic design and colors is deliberate and helps build consistency of identification.

Used Car Office

As with the exterior of the showroom, the intention here was to deliberately un-design the building. Accordingly, the architectural background was neutralized with suitable paint colors. The sign on the fascia is also similar to the dealer name identification above the showroom. The A-mark and descriptive nomenclature are given a horizontal treatment. The words "Select Used Cars" appear in white against a black background.

Used Car Lot Signage

A series of signs has been erected in strategic locations throughout the used car lot. On these the marketing slogan "Select Used Cars", lettered in white against a black field, appears beneath the A-mark. Purpose of these signs is to help build recognition for the slogan, to re-inforce the overall identity system, and to define the extent of the lot.

Before passing to the interior of the Grosse Pointe dealership facility, it should be noted that the new design format, when illuminated after dark, is extremely effective.

Interior Design

Intelligent space planning is extremely important if a dealer is to attain maximum utilization of his facility. Therefore, before embarking on an interior design program, an extensive survey was conducted of physical facilities. These were carefully analyzed for the most advantageous, or sales generating, use of space, and the findings were incorporated into the basic design plan.

Showroom and Offices

The one over-riding principle behind the total dealership design concept was to create for American Motors a selling atmosphere in which the products, and only the products, would be the featured attractions. Thus, in the re-design of the showroom and offices, and in the use of lighting, carpeting and wall treatment, our basic concern was to neutralize the environment so that the visual excitement of the cars themselves would be shown to maximum advantage.

Lighting

Stage lighting was employed to produce the kind of illuminative effects that would not only highlight the products at their various locations throughout the showroom but also emphasize, rather than obstruct, the clean lines of their distinctive styling.

Ceiling

Painted black to emphasize the stage lighting effect, minimize the general illumination, and give a uniform appearance to the various types of ceilings that exist throughout the dealership network.

Flooring

Dark carpeting, purposely neutral in tone, was installed to allow for perfect contrast with the colorful products.

Wall Treatment

Here again, subdued neutral colors have been used so as not to intrude or distract attention from the featured performers, the cars themselves.

Closing Offices

Specially designed movable cubicles, tailored for both men and women customers, to be used when finalizing the transaction. These are coated on the outside with a special metallic finish that supplies added product emphasis by reflecting the images of the new cars that are strategically positioned nearby. Colorful carpeting is used inside the closing rooms where it will not compete with the products. The decor, while comfortable and businesslike, is also stylish and makes a positive fashion statement particularly appealing to women.

Sales Manager's Office

Like the closing offices, its exterior too is coated in a metallic finish for heightened product emphasis. Reflective glass was installed to permit the manager to view the showroom floor without leaving his desk. Again, the office and furnishings are eminently functional, and typical of other executive offices and furnishings.

Customers' Lounge

In terms of customer convenience, particularly with women drivers, a suitable waiting area is of paramount importance. Here the decor is functional but inviting. Chairs are modern, austere in shape, and made of moulded plastic. A special incandescent light fixture illuminates the decorative modern graphics on the walls. The total effect is one of style, timeliness and relaxed, tasteful comfort.

Service Write-Up Area

As is the case with other parts of the building, this area has also been designed on a functional basis.

Interior Design continued

Write-Up Desk   A central feature of the Service Write-Up area is the new modular Write-Up Desk,
                        also finished with a metallic surface to reflect surrounding graphics. A wide red
                        stripe that runs across the floor from the base of the desk to the far wall tells the
                        motorist exactly where to stop his car.

Wall Graphics   These also play an integral role. One wall is painted in black to supply background
                        identification of customer write-up desk, lounge, cashier, etc., which appear in
                        contrasting white letters. The far wall also utilizes a black background, but displays
                        decorative graphics -- a series of attractive color wedges -- that add a bright, cheery,
                        modern touch to the entire area. This wall treatment, though inexpensive, appeals to
                        women and younger customers especially.

Service Department   Even here, in a place the customer seldom gets to see, the functional design strategy
                        is plainly in evidence. Up to man-door height, the walls of the service department
                        are shaded in a neutral gray tone for easy surface maintenance. Above this point,
                        the room is finished in light-reflecting white for improved visibility in the working area.

A. Primary Signage

The primary sign components are to be the
most prominently displayed. These signs
will read American Motors in matte white
upper and lower case bold Helvetica letters
on a matte black background and a red,
white and blue A-Mark.

Sizes

A. Double Face 4'0" wide by 30'0" high.
B. Double Face 4'0" wide by 24'0" high.
C. Double Face 5'6" wide by 38'0" high.
D. Double Face 5'6" wide by 33'0" high.

Double Face 4'0" wide by 30'0" high.

Double Face 4'0" wide by 24'0" high.

Double Face 5'6" wide by 38'0" high.

Double Face 5'6" wide by 33'0" high.

B. Dealer Name Signage (Fascia)

These signs will have the dealership name
in matte white upper and lower case bold
Helvetica letter on a matte black background
and a red, white and blue A-Mark. In most
installations the black background will
continue the entire length of the fascia
providing continuity of design. The following
sizes and mountings are available:

1. Illuminated
a. 2'0" high by various widths.
b. 4'0" high by various widths.
2. Non-Illuminated
a. 2'0" high by various widths.
b. 4'0" high by various widths.

a. 2'0" high by various widths.

b. 4'0" high by various widths.

FORMAT

Binding

Because the manual must anchor the program but be adaptable for changes made, it is wise to set it up in a loose-leaf binder. That way, any deletions or additions can be made easily by supplying all those with manuals with new pages to insert into the binder. This is also a safe holder for the reproduction art whether they be the originals sent with the loose leaf or new art sent as more are needed or as different sizes are generated. The binder's hard cover will prevent the art from bending or cracking, and no art can be torn if removed properly from the case.

United Bank of Virginia recognizes the efficiency of this format on the first page of its manual, as shown on the following page. This company's manual, designed by John Alcott, Jr., is progressive on all fronts. Another beneficial feature of the book is that estimated charges for specific items is included for all printed material for varying quantities. This gives the people involved a basis for cost controls as well as quality controls. For example, on the pages for business cards, the following information is included:

> One time charge for Layout Revision: $3.50 for relocating telephone on master die, plus $7.00 to $11.00 for each revised name and title imprint.
>
> Engraving charges: $35.00 for 250 cards, $48.50 for 500 cards (Substantial savings may be realized over these individual lot prices by placing orders for a number of individual lots at one time.).[1]

The practice of putting cost specifications into the manual has its advantages and disadvantages. If a specific supplier and his costs are mentioned, the supplier will often print the page for nothing and supply several free samples or extras of the pieces when they are ordered. However, putting in the price dates the manual page quickly, especially with spiralling paper costs, and it ties the company down to one supplier. If the manual is laid out in a looseleaf format and the company is willing to reprint or amend pages when prices change, this might be a good practice. Another way of handling the price specifications is to give an acceptable range, which allows the use of more than one supplier. This can be updated by sending out an additional sheet with new prices whenever area suppliers raise their prices.

[1] Specifications as of May 1969.

This manual describes the basic elements, policies and procedures employed in the implementation of the visual communications program of the United Virginia banks. This program has been thoughtfully developed to achieve maximum operational efficiencies and maximum public communications effectiveness . . . the overall objective being increased competitive advantage for all UVB member banks.

This manual is a continually expanding volume. New pages will be provided from time to time to supplement or replace those of the initial edition. Your cooperation in maintaining this valuable reference in an up-to-date form is essential.

PROCEDURE FOR USE

1. **Before independently developing any required item,** check the appropriate sections of this manual to see if an item is already available which meets your requirements.

2. **If item is not included in manual,** check with UVB Marketing Division as to whether the item is one of several currently under development and about to be incorporated on supplemental pages.

3. **If item is not currently under development,** UVB Marketing Division stands ready, upon request, to provide assistance in the development of any specific item or identification application.

4. **If you choose to develop an item independently,** utilize the elements and follow the policies as presented in the first two sections of this manual.

5. **Samples of all items developed independently** of UVB Marketing Division should be submitted for approval prior to being introduced to the public. This procedure has two purposes. First, it assures all UVB member banks that no individual bank will issue non-conforming materials which would tend to jeopardize the effectiveness of their own efforts. Second, and perhaps far more important, it will enable the Marketing Division to prepare and distribute supplemental pages so that all member banks may benefit from the creative thinking of the originating bank.

Length

The manual should be long enough to include all necessary information; not longer, not shorter. The beauty of the manual is that it lays out the needed material in a convenient manner. This ease of reference should not be interfered with by the inclusion of irrelevant information or embellishments, or by the exclusion of pertinent information.

For some companies, the proper length can be a few pages; for others, the manual can be quite long. Again, it all depends on the complexity of the program, the design, and the number of areas affected. It will also depend on who does the ordering, as discussed in the section on architecture and signage.

In the next part of this chapter, we have included three sample manuals. They vary greatly in length. The manual for Liberty Tree Mall, designed by Gregory Fossella Associates, is only two pages long. It includes all pertinent information for use of the mall's signature by stores in the mall, and gets this information into the two pages. Any other aspects of the program are either irrelevant for store owners, or do not exist. They therefore have provided a sound manual without wasting the precious time of the store managers. The manual format for the Bell System, however, is quite long even without the artwork. The information is extensive, complex, and necessary to the successful operation of the program. This, therefore, is also a sound format for a manual.

Typography

Because it represents the design system of the company, it would be nice for the manual to be set in beautifully designed type in an eye-catching layout. However, this is not necessary and may add needlessly to the cost of the program. As long as the pages are easy to read, clear of superfluous lines or type, and highlight the beginning of each section, the manual will serve its purpose.

If the book is set into type, an easy-to-read, good-sized type should be used. Headings and body copy should appear in the same area of the page on all pages, in order to avoid searching and a disorganized appearance. If the book is typed rather than set, the typing should be done on a clean typewriter so that no letters will fill in. Double spaces between the lines will make the reading easiest on the eyes.

Goodwill Industries set up and printed their own manual on a limited budget following Selame Design's guidelines, typing the textual matter and having the artwork representations and the headlines done by the designer. As simple as it is, it adequately provides the national direction and controls needed. This manual is shown in the next section of this chapter.

Whatever the format of the manual, the key word is functional. If the manual is not laid out to serve this purpose, the whole identity program can be undermined. After going through the entire identity program process, it makes no sense to waste that effort now. The manual deserves the same amount of attention as any other aspect of the program for this reason. And remember, it is better to have even a small, simple manual than to have no manual at all.

Sample Manuals

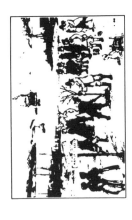

LIBERTY TREE MALL

INTRODUCTION

The purpose of this graphic system folder is to provide standards for use of the Liberty Tree Mall's signature. A great deal of time and effort has gone into developing this signature, so that stores within the Mall will have a strong graphic identification tool for use mainly in advertising, but also in any other applications where Liberty Tree Mall identification is required.

BACKGROUND

The Liberty Tree, our country's first symbol of freedom, was planted in 1646. Located in front of a grocery shop on the southeast corner of Washington and Essex streets, it became a gathering place for "The Sons of Liberty." This revolutionary organization was notified of meetings by means of a flag displayed in the Liberty Tree's branches and effigies of persons favoring the Stamp Act were also exhibited in its foliage. After flourishing for 119 years, the tree was cut down during the British siege of Boston.

The Liberty Tree sculpture that stands in the center of the Mall was designed for the 1964 New York World's Fair. It stood in the New England Pavilion before coming back to Boston.

SYMBOL

The symbol or face to our name is a strong, contemporary interpretation of the Liberty Tree described above. Boston Industrial Design consultants, Gregory Fossella Associates, have developed this symbol to capture the key visual features of the Liberty Tree sculpture. At the same time, it projects a warm, femininely-attractive image to the public.

LOGOTYPE

The words "Liberty Tree Mall" in the signature utilize a hand-drawn, specially-designed letter form. It is not a standard typeface and no one should attempt to re-draw it. The letter style is a balance of old and new, skillfully combined to create a unique logotype.

SIGNATURE

Two versions of the Liberty Tree Mall signature (combination of symbol & logotype) have been approved for use. One version is on three lines, forming a square area. The other is on one line. Either is acceptable, so use whichever one fits a particular layout the best.

You'll find both styles included on a reproduction sheet in this folder, in the different sizes you'll probably need. Extra copies of repro sheets may be obtained from Pearson Weiss MacDonald Inc., 171 Newbury Street, Boston, Mass. 02116.

COLOR

The Liberty Tree Mall signature is shown to its best advantage in two-color printing using red and blue on a white background to give a patriotic effect. Red and blue swatches for visual color matching have been included in this folder. The recommended red is PMS-192; the recommended blue, PMS-286. The symbol should always be red and the logotype always blue whenever these two colors are available. When PMS inks are not available, a visual match should be made.

Two-color uses are shown opposite. But more often than not two colors will not be available. In this case the logotype should appear in a solid color with the symbol a 60% screen of the color used. Newspaper ads are a prime example of this type of usage.

CONCLUSION

It's important to this identification program that no symbols, signatures, logotypes or colors other than those supplied in this folder be used for Liberty Tree Mall. This manual represents a major undertaking to provide the graphic tools necessary to create and maintain a strong and consistent graphic image for Liberty Tree Mall. Adherence to these guidelines will benefit everyone associated with the Mall, and we ask the full cooperation of all persons, companies and agencies connected with the graphic design decisions involving use of the Liberty Tree Mall signature. For further information or help on special problems that arise, please contact Pearson Weiss MacDonald.

History

Over the years, the official symbol of
Goodwill Industries has been the Goodwill
seal.
Good Willy has been another.
A major step in upgrading the image of
Goodwill is being taken with the
"Smiling G".

Our Symbol

After testing and studies, the new
Smiling G was created. It is designed
to fulfill three basic needs:
Recognition, memorability and funtional
adaptability.

It is legally protected, and must not
be tampered with.

**Purpose of
Symbol and
Color Control**

Our most important asset is a strong
identity, and this identity is possible
through an organized, controlled
program.

The following pages will show the
Smiling G identity system. It consists
of the following items...

(a) Symbol control sheet
(b) Color control cards
(c) Do's and Don'ts on symbol and color
    use
(d) Letterhead design
(e) Envelope (no. 10) design
(f) Business Card design
(g) Goodwill Bag design
(h) Store Sign design
(i) Collection Box design
(j) Vehicle design

Symbol Control

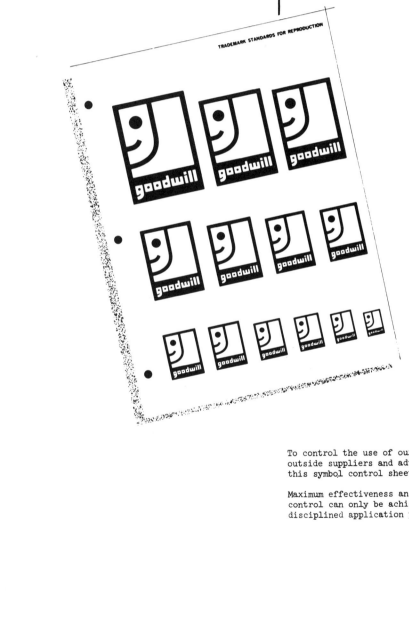

To control the use of our mark by all outside suppliers and advertising media, this symbol control sheet was created.

Maximum effectiveness and copyright control can only be achieved through a disciplined application program.

TRADEMARK STANDARDS FOR REPRODUCTION

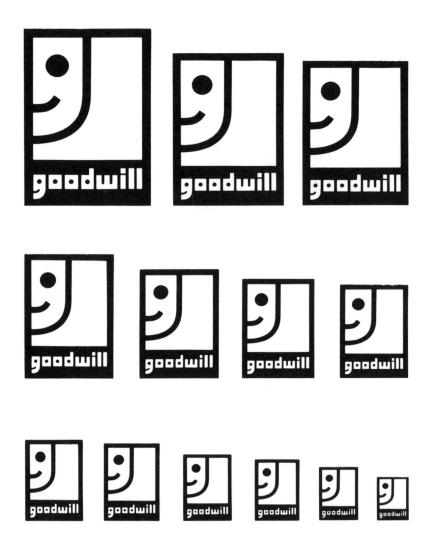

Color Control

Color too is an inportant part of our overall identity program. Our house colors were created with the same care as the mark itself.

Color control cards like these insure a consistency in color in literature, packaging and architecture. Colors are PMS Process Blue and PMS 106 Yellow.

DO'S and DON'TS

DON'T substitute color or guess.

DON'T mutilate or ornament the symbol.

DO follow official colors, give color chips to supplier.

Do use printed trademark sheet for reproduction of mark and lettering in every case.

Most of all

Remember:

Our image is our key to a high public reputation. Goodwill has invested in making this image one of the finest in the world...so make good use of it and use it with pride.

Letterhead

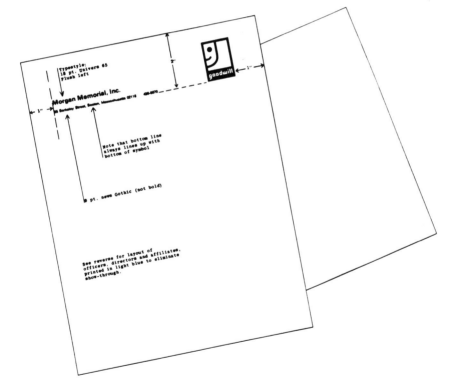

Envelope, No. 10

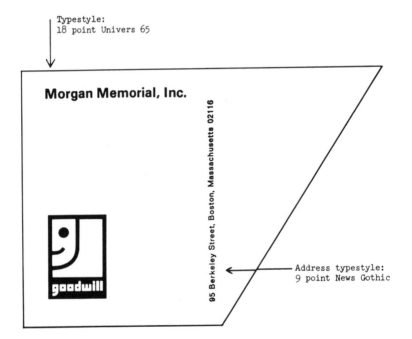

Typestyle:
18 point Univers 65

Morgan Memorial, Inc.

95 Berkeley Street, Boston, Massachusetts 02116

goodwill

Address typestyle:
9 point News Gothic

Business Card

HOWARD A. PATTERSON
PUBLIC RELATIONS DIRECTOR

MORGAN MEMORIAL. INC.
GOODWILL INDUSTRIES
95 BERKELEY STREET.
BOSTON. MASS. 02116   426-9670

Note that bottom line squares
with bottom of symbol. ————————→

Note that all type
flushes left.

Typestyle: News Gothic Extended

Exact size and location of symbol.
Reproduced from repro sheet.

Bag

Identification

Our Goodwill Bag is the vehicle in which contributors place their donations and a means for us to say Thank you.

Its appearance must be clean and neat with copy kept at a minimum. The message, "For pick-up of large articles call", followed by phone numbers appear on the side of bag.

Store

Identity

Store identity should be direct and
colorful. This sign says all we want
and need to say.

The

Collection

Cénter

Coloring and lettering of our collection boxes
should, again, be clean and neat.

Use blue lettering on a yellow background.
Use yellow lettering on a blue background.

Paint colors are: Blue--DuPont # 93-98587;
Yellow--DuPont # 93-9854H.

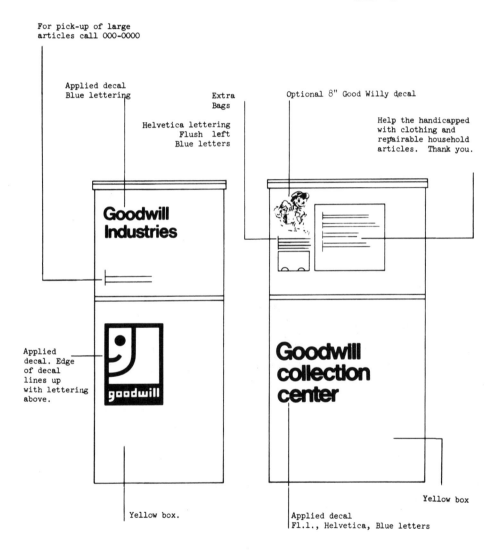

All lettering is
Helvetica typestyle
Flush left
Blue on yellow
Yellow on blue

For pick-up of large
articles call 000-0000

Applied decal
Blue lettering

Extra
Bags

Optional 8" Good Willy decal

Helvetica lettering
Flush left
Blue letters

Help the handicapped
with clothing and
repairable household
articles. Thank you.

Applied
decal. Edge
of decal
lines up
with lettering
above.

Yellow box.

Yellow box

Applied decal
Fl.l., Helvetica, Blue letters

All lettering is
Helvetica typestyle
Flush left
Blue on yellow
Yellow on blue

Roof, yellow

Applied decal
Blue lettering
Flush left
Helvetica typestyle

Applied
symbol

Help the handicapped
with clothing and
repairable household
articles. Thank you.

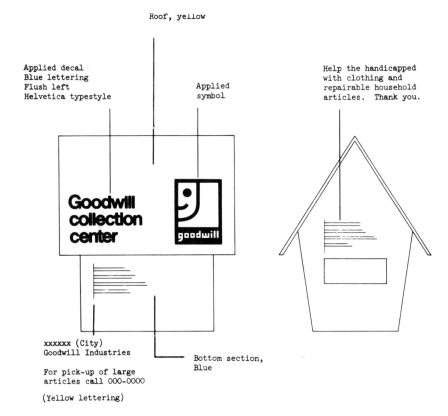

xxxxxx (City)
Goodwill Industries

For pick-up of large
articles call 000-0000

(Yellow lettering)

Bottom section,
Blue

Vehicle
Identity

A well designed truck makes people take a second look. We recommend that the bottom half and cab be blue. The top half should be painted yellow.

Lettering should be blue on yellow; yellow on blue.

Paint colors are identical to collection boxes: Blue DuPont #93-98587; Yellow DuPont #93-9854H.

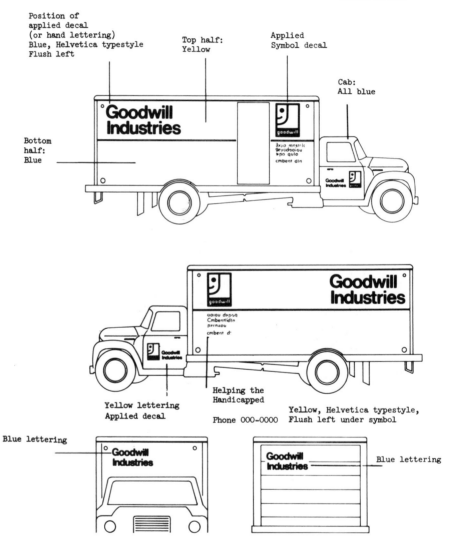

All lettering is
Helvetica typestyle
Flush left
Blue on yellow
Yellow on blue

Position of
applied decal
(or hand lettering)
Blue, Helvetica typestyle
Flush left

Top half:
Yellow

Applied
Symbol decal

Cab:
All blue

Bottom
half:
Blue

Goodwill Industries

Helping the
Handicapped
Phone 000-0000

Yellow lettering
Applied decal

Yellow, Helvetica typestyle,
Flush left under symbol

Blue lettering

Blue lettering

THE BELL SYSTEM CORPORATE MANUAL FORMAT[2]

I. Introduction
    A. History of the Bell seal
        1. Old design.
        2. Modifications, 1889-1939.
    B. Visual symbol of the Bell System
        1. Symbol is no longer limited in association to simply
            the telephone.
        2. It is now a visual symbol for entire Bell System, its
            companies, its products, and its services. Public un-
            derstanding.
    C. The legal aspect
        Proper and consistent use will protect mark.
    D. Better public understanding
        Based on the use of words and name relationships.
        Visual relationships for quick recognition.
    E. Public relations and marketing aspects
        Need for a consistent look.
    F. The system of identification
        Consists of:
        1. Standards of *name* relationships (descriptive phrases
            that relate companies, products, and services to the
            Bell System).
        2. Standards of *visual* relationships (visual
            arrangements of the graphic elements of iden-
            tification).
    G. Elements of identification
        1. The Bell seal.
        2. Type specifications.
        3. Signature formats.
        4. Standard color.
    H. The Bell System look
        1. Consistent use of elements.

---

[2]. This format was written by students in a graphic design class at Northeastern
University as an exercise in designing identity manuals. It is not the actual Bell System
manual or format and was not written in conjunction with Bell. It is included to show the initial stage of a very complex manual for large companies.

        2. Style and layout of *all* visual material should accurately reflect goals and standards that characterize the System.

  I. Coordinator of corporate identification

        1. Each company has elected a public relations coordinator of corporate identification to administer and coordinate the program and to give guidance and direction when needed.

        2. List of current company coordinators.

  J. Holders of manual

        1. Held by people having an active interest in company identification practices.

        2. Kept up to date (sheets forwarded by coordinator).

        3. If holder transferred, manual shall remain on premises.

        4. Holder is to return manual if not needed.

II. The Bell Seal

  A. Proper seal shown with an explanation of how it is to be used, in which media, and so on

        1. One color must *always* be used: blue preferred, other colors acceptable in some applications.

        2. Background: *always* one color (same color inside and outside of circle).

  B. Positive and negative

        1. May be used in both forms.

        2. Never used by applying it in positive on a dark background or in negative on a light one.

  C. No other graphic elements

        1. Background (patches, lines, etc.).

        2. Seal must *never* be used as promotional symbol, on information maps, etc.

  D. Positioning

    Always parallel to the other elements (wrong and correct samples shown).

  E. Reproduction of seal

        1. Must *never* be traced, etc.

        2. Must *always* be reproduced from an authorized original.

        3. Examples of minimum size of seal to be used for letterpress printing on:

      a. Newsprint stock—100%(solid), 80% tint, 50% tint,
and 20% tint. All tints shown in a #55 and a #65
screen.

      b. #1 coated stock (tints shown in a #110 screen).

    4. Offset printing.

      a. #1 sulphite bond (tints shown in a #150 screen).

      b. Vellum finish (tints shown in a #133 screen).

      c. #1 offset enamel (tints shown in a #85 screen).

    5. Silk screen printing.
Examples of smallest seals to be used on Kromkote,
cover stock, and text stock.

    6. "Bell System"—omitted.
If reproduced in smaller sizes than shown, the words
Bell System should be omitted. Only applies where
the technical limitations of a particular reproduction
method prevent faithful and complete reproduction
of seal. (Examples shown.)

F. Three-dimensional seals
Provides a more dramatic image of dignity, quality, and
permanence.

G. Fabricating three-dimensional seals

    1. Maximum thickness.

    2. Special problems if background shows through (examples shown).

    3. Mounting of seal (examples).

H. Lighting and contrast considerations
Examples of correct background to use so that mark is
not distorted by lighting, shadows, etc.

I. Special display effects
Examples shown.

J. Use of more than one seal

    1. One seal to be used at all times.

    2. Acceptable for safety paper or envelope lining only.

K. Radii for developing bottom of bell, letters, and three
rings within bell
Examples and dimensions shown.

L. Type specifications

    1. Type face.

      a. Standard type face must always be used.

      b. Lighter weights may be used when necessary.

c. Reason for choice (distinctive shapes).
2. Upper and lower case letters.
   a. Reasons for.
   b. Examples.
   c. Caps used only on lettering in bell symbol.
3. Type specifications for signature (examples shown).
4. Letter spacing (examples).
5. Word spacing (examples).
6. Lighter weights.
   a. Appropriate uses: stationary, business forms, directory covers.
   b. Examples in Univers 47, 57, and 67 (typeface).
7. Typographical optics.
   Proper spacing (examples).

III. Company Signatures
   A. Standards of name relationship
      1. It is essential that the relationships between the companies in the Bell System be clearly defined.
      2. Examples showing proper identification of companies in the system.
   B. Definition of a signature
   C. Signature evaluation
      Clearer communications will result if each company evaluates the way its name appears in its signature.
   D. Size relationships between seal and company names
      1. Examples of proper sizes.
      2. A feeling of authority suggested by a large seal.
   E. Layout options for company signatures
      1. Seal may appear on either side, above, or below signature (examples).
      2. Never split (examples).
   F. Use of signatures in general application
      1. Should not be jammed into a layout as an afterthought (examples).
      2. Should be given generous space so sponsor of each ad is recognized (examples).

IV. Bell System Blue
   A. Blue as a tradition
      First seal designed 1880.
   B. Need for a standard

Needed to help give consistency to overall corporate look.

C. Use of Bell blue

Strongly considered for use of bell seal when used in formal and semiformal applications.

D. Use of other colors

Acceptable when necessary (motor vehicles).

E. Characteristics of Bell blue

1. Designed for use with white.
2. Versatile with any background.

F. Bell blue formulas

1. Coated paper.
2. Uncoated paper.
3. Color specification sheets.

V. Building Identification

A. General

1. Should state clearly, simply, tastefully, and consistently to whom the building belongs.
2. Responsibility for administering program lies with building engineering group and coordinator of corporate identification.

B. Buildings to be identified

All, except where not permitted by local codes or ordinances or for security reasons.

C. Information shown

1. Correct seal and company name (always).
2. Relationship of company to System.
3. Purpose of building (garage).

D. Ordering information

Seals, letters, and approved colors available from Western Electric.

E. No special effects

Mark never distorted.

F. Approved seal

1. Never to be altered.
2. No maps or other graphic shapes.

G. Approved typography (examples)

H. Company signature considerations

1. Complete signature always shown on same side of building—never split.

2. If high-rise building, seal alone is enough (where space is limited).

I. Company names
   Always complete enough so there is no doubt.

J. Muti-signature signs
   When subsidiaries are housed together, the one that occupies greater portion of building may be listed first.

K. Descriptive phrases
   1. Key part of corporate program.
   2. Used whenever possible.

L. Building purpose
   Words showing this information should be meaningful as possible.

M. Color
   Keep approved format.

N. Four types of approved signs (examples)

O. Plaques
   Permissible in residential neighborhoods where more modest signs are needed (three examples shown).

P. Free-standing signs
   1. Permissible when face of building provides undesirable background.
   2. Building is set off street.
   3. Road where building is not easily seen.
   4. Placed near traffic flow and distance viewing.

Q. Special signs
   Permissible when others are not accepted.

VI. Coin Telephone Signs
   A. Introduction
      Reasons for proper usage.

   B. Objectives of program
      1. Established format for family look.
      2. Insure replacement of improper signs.
      3. Create a system for more tasteful and effective sign placement.
      4. Indicate clearly that installations are Bell System's.

   C. Advantages
      1. Improved customer recognition.
      2. Reduction in visual clutter across the country.
      3. Improved public service image.

    D. Role of corporate identification
       Important for customers to know when they are using
       Bell equipment.
    E. Design elements
       Simple, legible from distance, distinctive, attractive,
       consistent in appearance.
    F. Three major areas of signing
       1. Showing location and direction.
       2. Signs on booth.
       3. Signs and markings on and near telephone in-
          truments.
    G. Signs showing location and direction
       Two examples (round and square).
    H. Nonilluminated applications
       1. Maximum viewing effectiveness.
       2. Vantage points and viewing distances.
       3. Always placed at right angles.
       4. Avoid redundant signing.
       5. Multiple signing if vantage points and viewing dis-
          tances are considered.
    I. Variations (examples)
VII. Directory Covers
    A. Introduction
    B. Functions of directory covers
       1. Should show clearly and simply certain basic infor-
          mation about directory and area covered.
       2. Should be tasteful and attractive enough to reflect
          positively on the company.
    C. Concept of total cover
       1. Front should give basic information.
       2. Back should relate in visual format to front cover.
    D. Front cover
       1. Need only give basic information.
       2. Who published.
       3. Where (area served).
       4. What (publication is).
       5. When (published).
       6. Correct examples of basic copy.
       7. Keep type at tasteful size; not overpowering (right
          and wrong examples).

        8. Examples showing right and wrong front covers (color).

    E. Yellow Pages emblem.
    Show in modest size so it does not dominate (examples).

    F. Back cover used for
        1. Merchandising messages.
        2. Public service messages.
        3. Helpful telephone information.
        4. Tasteful continuation of front cover illustration.
        5. Uncluttered.
        6. Examples, good and bad.

    G. Backbone
        1. Should quickly identify book.
        2. Colors should harmonize with front and back covers.
        3. Legibility important (texture of paper).

    H. Total graphic format
    Front, back, and backbone.

    I. Emblem of Yellow Pages
        1. Official emblem is only one to be used.
        2. May be used wherever additional information is needed (other than Yellow Page service; for example, stationary and so on).

    J. Use of color
        1. Always used in consistent form.
        2. Examples showing proper usage.

    K. Typography
        1. Use of (examples).
        2. Exceptions (examples).
        3. Use of combined, adjacent graphic elements (examples).
        4. Distortion of (examples).

    L. Logos
        1. Specification sheets for reproduction.
        2. Color specification sheets.

VIII.   Exhibits and Displays
    A. General
        1. Always clear.
        2. Quickly recognized.

    B. Need for early planning
    Symbol crowded and not easily identified.

    C. Misuse of seal
       Background inside and outside of ring always the same (right and wrong examples).
    D. Multiple use of seal
       1. Vantage points (examples).
       2. Viewing distances (examples).
       3. Traffic approaches (examples).
    E. Use of station number cards (examples).
  IX. Other Application—Flags and Pennants
    A. Provide additional means of corporate identification
    B. Optional
    C. American flag given preference
    D. Examples
  X. Vehicle Markings
    A. General
       For quick recognition of seal and company name.
    B. Vehicle markings
       Seal and upper and lower case letters in company name.
    C. Color and source of supply of markings
       1. Gold on green, which provides a rich, effective contrast.
       2. Available through Western Electric.
    D. Legal requirements
       1. Information re maximum load and gross weight.
       2. Up to three feet high in black so as not to be confused as part of signature.
       3. Garage location (if required).
    E. Posters
       One to a vehicle (examples).
    F. Vehicle types: cab and body (examples)
    G. Vehicle types: special (examples)
    H. Vehicle types: passenger cars (examples)
    I. Vehicle types: compact vans
       1. Examples.
       2. Only on flat surfaces, sharp contours distort identification.
    J. Vehicle types: tractor trailers (examples)
    K. Arrangement of long names
       Same as noted in section on "Company Signatures" (examples).

XI. Trademarks and Service Marks
  A. Introduction
  B. Always use mark as adjective; tells reader brand
  C. Always use correct common name
     Specific, not general.
  D. Always make a mark distinctive
     1. To set apart and to help it function as a "brand" name.
     2. Treat differently from common name.
  E. Always show registration (registered)
     1. Proper use.
     2. Registration symbol.
     3. If unregistered, show same as registered except omit mark.

XII. Stationery and Business Forms
   Acceptable and unacceptable (photographs)

Appendix

Sources of Information

Rather than pay money for market research that has already been done, the company can look into several sources of information that will give the pertinent data or let you know where it can be found. Also, whenever a corporate identity program is being initiated, a local or national trade association can give you a great wealth of information on the marketplace, designers, architects, and so on. These organizations, their publications, or the publications with which they are affiliated should not be overlooked at any time. When planning a new corporate identity or just during the normal course of business, a trade association is a center of information, helps the industry's relationship with government and can keep you posted on the latest ordinances, helps the industry's public relations, does its own market research that it shares with its members, and has meetings and conventions that bring you together with other members of your trade. Besides the information the conventions yield through their workshops and general conversations, the associations can give you other information: uniform accounting procedures, the latest business statistics in general and for your field, market research in the area and in the nation, and information on accepted business practices and ethics.

To belong to a trade organization and not to take advantage of these services can lead to wasted time, energy, and money. The list that follows gives the names, addresses, and telephone numbers of several of the better-known associations. Also included are the names of several private organizations and research groups and the names of professional organizations, which would be a good source for looking into advertising, architectural, and design firms. This list is by no means complete, but it is a start. Often, if some organization on this list cannot help you, they will know who can.

TRADE ORGANIZATIONS

American Booksellers Association Inc.
800 Second Avenue
New York, N.Y. 10017
212-867-9060

American Bankers Association
1120 Connecticut Avenue NE
Washington, D.C. 20036
202-467-4000

American Footwear Institute
1611 N. Kent Street
Arlington, VA. 22209
703-522-8070

American Retail Association Executives
Chamber of Commerce Building
New Kensington, PA. 15068
412-339-6616

American Retail Federation
1616 H Street NW
Washington D.C. 20006
202-783-7971

American Savings and Loan Institute
111 East Wacker Drive
Chicago, IL. 60601
312-644-3100

Brand Names Foundation, Inc.
477 Madison Avenue
New York, N.Y. 10022
212-753-4131

International Association of Chain Stores
1028 Connecticut Avenue
Washington, D.C. 20036
202-659-1141

International Council of Shopping Centers
445 Park Avenue
New York, N.Y. 10022
212-594-5130

International Franchise Association
1025 Connecticut Avenue NW Ste. 906
Washington, D.C. 20036
202-833-9098

Mass Retailing Institute
570 Seventh Avenue
New York, N.Y. 10018
212-354-6600

National Association of Chain Drug Stores
1911 Jefferson Davis Highway
Arlington, VA. 22202
703-521-1144

National Association of College Stores
55 E. College Street
Oberlin, OH. 44074
216-775-1561

National Association of Convenience Stores
1835 K Street NW
Washington, D.C. 20006

National Association of Display Industries
120 East 34th Street Ste. 2J
New York, N.Y. 10016
212-682-0447

National Association of Food Chains
1725 I Street NW
Washington, D.C. 20006
202-338-7822

National Association of Independent Food Retailers
427 Board of Trade Building
Portland, OR. 97204

National Association of Mass Merchandisers
1612 K Street N.W.
Washington, D.C. 20006

National Association of Mutual Savings Banks
200 Park Avenue
New York, N.Y. 10017
212-973-4720

National Association of Retail Druggists
One East Wacker Drive
Chicago, IL. 60601
312-321-1146

National Association of Retail Grocers of the United States
2000 Spring Road Ste. 620
Oakbrook, IL. 60521
312-654-1955

National Association of Sign and Display Advertisers
600 Hunter Drive
Oakbrook, IL. 60521
312-242-0920

National Association of Store Fixture Manufacturers
53 W. Jackson Boulevard
Chicago, IL. 60604
312-922-0509

National Association of Truck Stop Operators, Inc.
501 Slatters Lane
Alexandria, VA. 22314
703-549-2100

National Association of Variety Stores
7646 W. Devon Avenue
Chicago, IL. 60631

National Electric Sign Association
600 Hunter Drive Ste. 305
Oakbrook, IL. 60521
312-323-3600

National Restaurant Association
1530 N. Lake Shore Drive
Chicago, IL. 60610
312-787-2525

National Retail Merchants Association
100 West 31st Street
New York, N.Y. 10001
212-244-8780

National Sporting Goods Association
717 N. Michigan Avenue
Chicago, IL. 60611
312-944-0205

Super Market Institute, Inc.
200 E. Ontario St.
Chicago, IL. 60611
312-664-4590

PROFESSIONAL ORGANIZATIONS

Advertising Club of New York
Park Avenue at 35th Street
New York, N.Y. 10016
212-685-1810

Advertising Research Foundation
3 East 54th Street
New York, N.Y. 10022
212-751-5656

Advertising & Sales Executives Club
913 Baltimore Avenue
Kansas City, MO. 64105
816-842-4030

American Advertising Federation
1225 Connecticut Avenue NW
Washington, D.C. 20036
202-659-1800

American Association of Advertising Agencies
200 Park Avenue
New York, N.Y. 10017
212-682-2500

American Institute of Architects
1785 Massachusetts Avenue N.W.
Washington, D.C. 20036
202-265-3113

American Institute of Graphic Arts
1059 Third Avenue
New York, N.Y. 10021
212-752-0813

American Institute of Interior Designers
730 Fifth Avenue Suite 1204
New York, N.Y. 10019
212-265-2090

American Marketing Association
222 S. Riverside Plaza
Chicago, IL. 60606
312-648-0536

Bank Marketing Association
309 W. Washington Street
Chicago, IL. 60606
312-782-1442

Bank Public Relations & Marketing Association
120 West Madison
Chicago, IL. 60602
312-782-1442

Direct Mail Advertising Association, Inc.
230 Park Avenue
New York, N.Y. 10017

Industrial Designers Society of America
541 E. 20th Street
New York, N.Y. 10010
212-246-5050

Institute of Outdoor Advertising
625 Madison Avenue
New York, N.Y. 10022
212-755-4157

Institute of Store Planners
415 East 53rd Street
New York, N.Y. 10022
212-753-5370

International Advertising Association, Inc.
475 Fifth Avenue
New York, N.Y. 10017
212-684-1583

National Society of Interior Designers
315 East 62nd Street
New York, N.Y. 10021
212-838-5906

Package Designers Council
299 Madison Avenue
New York, N.Y. 10017
212-682-1980

Point-of-Purchase Advertising Institute
521 Fifth Avenue
New York, N.Y. 10017
212-682-7041

Premium Advertising Association of America
366 Madison Avenue Ste. 700
New York, N.Y. 10017
212-867-2060

Public Relations Society of America
845 Third Avenue
New York, N.Y. 10022

Sales & Marketing Executives International
630 Third Avenue
New York, N.Y. 10017
212-986-9300

Sales Executives Club of New York
Hotel Roosevelt
New York, N.Y. 10017
212-689-5117

Sales Promotion Executives Association
2130 Delancey Place
Philadelphia, PA. 19103
215-732-9340

Savings Institutions Marketing Society of America
111 E. Wacker Drive
Chicago, IL. 60601

Specialty Advertising Association
740 North Rush Street
Chicago, IL. 60611
312-944-3301

Television Bureau of Advertising
1 Rockefeller Center
New York, N.Y. 10020
212-757-9420

United States Trademark Association
6 East 45th Street
New York, N.Y. 10017
212-986-5880

PRIVATE ORGANIZATIONS AND RESEARCH GROUPS

Advanced Management Research, Inc.
1370 Avenue of the Americas
New York, N.Y. 10019
212-765-6400

American Management Association
135 West 50th Street
New York, N.Y. 10020
212-586-8100

The Conference Board
845 Third Avenue
New York, N.Y. 10022
212-759-0900

Management Horizons
1651 NW Professional Plaza
Columbus, OH. 43220
614-457-7250

Marketing Sciences Institute
14 Story Street
Cambridge, MS. 02139
617-491-2060

Newspaper Advertising Bureau
485 Lexington Avenue
New York, N.Y. 10017
212-557-1800

SAMI (Selling Areas-Marketing, Inc.)
1290 Avenue of the Americas
New York, N.Y. 10019
212-556-4206

Index